REALITY
AND
THE HEROIC
PATTERN

Last Plays of
Ibsen, Shakespeare, and Sophocles

REALITY AND THE HEROIC PATTERN

Last Plays of
Ibsen, Shakespeare, and Sophocles

by David Grene

The University of Chicago Press

CHICAGO AND LONDON

PN
1623
G7

SBN: 226–30788-3 (clothbound); 226–30789-1 (paperback)
Library of Congress Catalog Card Number: 67-25519
THE UNIVERSITY OF CHICAGO PRESS, CHICAGO 60637
The University of Chicago Press, Ltd., London

56048

Preface

These essays are the outcome of a number of courses I have given in the University of Chicago on these plays. It was only gradually that I came to feel how curious are the connections between them. At first I was aware of the obvious fact that all of them except *Ajax* (which I look on as a preview of the two later plays I have treated) were the last written by their respective authors, and that certain of them, notably *When We Dead Awaken, The Tempest,* and (in a sense) *Oedipus at Colonus,* are almost transparently concerned with the author's farewell to his work. I gradually saw that in each instance the last plays formed a kind of series, with certain common features of plot and treatment, and a similar theme. Finally I came to feel that the theme itself was alike enough to make it interesting to discuss the ten plays in a single volume.

That theme at its most direct—as in the Ibsen plays—is the establishment of meaning for the events of a life, looking backward from its conclusion. If we refuse to see these events as "happenings" culminating in a last "happening," we try to discover their "meaning." This is to relate the sequence of acts to some pattern of reality (as far as we can grasp it), so that we can see some things as having led us right and others wrong; so that we believe there was a direction and a significance to our lives. In Ibsen it is what was wrong that impressed him. These plays of his deal with the winning for the life of the hero of a deeper meaning, which is a superior reality to that of the mistakes.

All such sequences of acts imply the medium in which they occur—time. So there is much about time in all of the plays, for the power of time alters the meaning of events and can even almost deny the objective existence of the acts. And much about death, since, in its denial of further experience, because the chart is at last drawn, it drives us to ask where the journey went. Thus the theme in Shakespeare broadens to embrace many of man's general efforts to establish continuity of understanding, an agreed meaning for events, even objects and forms that will defeat mass anonymity and death. The central tragic question, not answered nearly so affirmatively as in Ibsen, is: which is the deeper reality, the standard of "ordinary" nature or the pattern that man has laid upon it or found in it? In Sophocles there are two standards again, but they are not nature and artifice; they are the human and the divine.

Ibsen's version is nearest to us in time, most familiar, but it is perhaps questionable whether it is nearest to us in feeling any more. It has much in common with nineteenth-century Romanticism. It is the defiance of death by making death itself the expression of what the hero believes to have been the greatest and most perfect elements in his life and character. As I suggest in the Ibsen essay, it is peculiarly a dramatist's idea of a suitable death. These plays are largely a brooding retrospect of errors and sins climaxed by the spectacular act of atonement. They are full of the certainty that there *is* the possibility of such an act of atonement that will alter the balance decisively. Such a death is the proof of the hero's integrity and his ability to see a certain truth in reality, a truth which is identical with his private vision of himself. Solness and Rubek are so vindicated, and the same truth condemns cowards like Allmers and his wife, and "dead" men—that is, men who have not learned the lesson of their failures—like Borkman.

Sophocles has presented the theme at its barest and most abstract. It is here simply a conflict between two realities, between two "meanings," that appropriate to the man that is (Ajax, Philoctetes, or Oedipus) and the semi-divinity of the hero-daemon that he is shortly to become. It deals with his human rights—to love his friends and hate his enemies, with the acts proper to these emotions—and the denial of these rights by the need to serve the more impersonal necessity of the gods' purposes. The plays are written almost altogether about the feelings of the man confronted with the something-that-will-be which both is, and is not, himself. They reflect an intense sense of the cruelty of the universe in which the hero finds himself a victim of the utilitarianism of his fellows, who will use him or discard him according to the serviceability of his divine appointment, and the paradoxical torture of the gods who punish or reward without human reason. To the cosmic meaning of the mysterious translation of the sinner-hero there is no key that Sophocles has certainly given.

In Shakespeare the stress on time, and death or translation, is different. It is not borne by the individual life, as in Ibsen or Sophocles. Personal death plays little part in these plots, and the notion of the Sophoclean translation is quite alien. But it would hardly be an exaggeration to describe these last plays as a prolonged dialogue between the values of nature and artifice as reflections of the truth of reality. In Shakespeare's time there were aspects of social and political and religious life which more truly showed belief in a kind of immortality than would be the case in Ibsen's nineteenth century or Sophocles' fifth-century Athens. So the plays deal with questions of the succession of sovereigns, the hereditariness of nobility in feeling, the functions of law. But what remains most in our minds—and perhaps what Shakespeare has emphasized most—is the relation of natural life and the versions of it that the artist in man makes in his images. There is the living statue of Hermione, the Arcadias and rural Utopias of *Cymbeline* and *Winter's Tale,* the masques in all three plays, finally the island of Caliban and Ariel against Prospero's renewed habitation of Milan. In all of these art tries to combine a fixed meaning with the fluidity of life, since fluid life carries death. Yet the answer to the question, Which is the truer reality? is a very hesitant one. The statue has wrinkles and indeed is a living woman; the Arcadias and Utopias are inhabited by people who do not find themselves immune to temptations and sufferings, any more than others; the masques are broken off when more serious matters supervene; Prospero *does* go back to Milan. The truest likeness of life is the stage and the stage demands the end of the play with its performance. Does death annihilate also the meaning? Life is drawn into the simile of the acting and the scenery becomes one with the objects it represents. What do we say to Prospero's

> and like the baseless fabric of this vision,
> the cloudcapped towers, the gorgeous palaces,
> the solemn temples, the great globe itself,
> yea, all which it inherit shall dissolve,
> and like this unsubstantial pageant faded
> leave not a wrack behind. We are such stuff
> as dreams are made on and our little life
> is rounded with a sleep.

To read these ten plays with such a theme in mind is not to establish any "philosophy of the dramatist," nor even those aspects of it that bear on social or religious life. It is to put oneself into the position of responding to the passionate significance of the plays—we hope, as their authors intended—to gain that moment of passionate intensity in which all worlds are denied except that inside which the dramatist holds us convinced of its truth. To be able to do this through the plays of three dramatists like these is, I believe, to deepen to a degree one's own sense of reality.

The classes with which I have discussed these plays are the source to which I owe most and to which I here express my gratitude. But there are four friends to whom some particular acknowledgments must be made—Saul Bellow, Hannah Arendt, and William and Shirley Letwin. They have read all these essays and helped by their comments, though perhaps most of all by their unfailing understanding and encouragement. I wish to thank Mr. Arthur Morey for valuable assistance in checking references and compiling the footnotes.

Unfortunately I do not know Norwegian and therefore my essays on Ibsen had to be based on English and German translations. Muriel Bradbrook's book convinced me how much I have lost in not knowing the original.

Thirty years of association with the University of Chicago, twenty of it on the staff of the Committee on Social Thought, have thoroughly driven home to me my deep sense of indebtedness to both.

Lastly, to my wife, Ethel, I owe an enormous debt for all sorts of help in writing this book.

Contents

Ibsen

Shakespeare

Sophocles

Ibsen

INTRODUCTION

In a letter to Count Prozor in 1900 Ibsen wrote of his last four plays—*The Master Builder, Little Eyolf, John Gabriel Borkman,* and *When We Dead Awaken* (which he called the Epilogue)—in the following words: "You are basically right in saying that the series which ended with the Epilogue actually started with *Master Builder*. But I do not wish to enlarge on this subject further."[1]

We may easily speculate on why the author did not want to discuss the common subject of the series, but a common subject, in some sense, Ibsen clearly thought they had. A plausible guess to account for his reticence might be that these plays came so directly out of his own experience and his own inner life that they were uncomfortable. They certainly imply a personal involvement in a problem and a personal commitment to a position. Perhaps it is because of this that they seem more important today than anything else he wrote. In a way, they seem the beginning of nearly all the modern problems in European literature.

In them Ibsen's theatrical self far transcended his own intellectual ability to understand the problems of the world and society as they are expressed in the formulations of the early and middle

1

plays. He may be theoretically a believer in the values of Stockman—I almost think that he was. He is certainly the opponent of Kroll. But it is only in the last plays that the depth of his personal feelings was mobilized, and so he took for his subject a dimension of life which he cannot express in simple intellectual terms, and which is truly heroic. Solness, Rubek, and Borkman are not only much bigger than the figures of the plays that preceded them,[2] they are quite unlike them.[3]

Ibsen was well over sixty when he wrote the first play of the "series." It is quite clear that the near approach of death is the sharpest stimulus to his thought. He was also haunted by the idea that his work had not expressed the fullness of what it was in him to give, either because art as such was the wrong road for him, or because he had been a bad artist. Somehow connected with what he viewed as the failure or defect of his creativity was his sexual unhappiness. The love affair with Emilia Bardach and the later relationship to the Norwegian pianist Anderson, both women very much younger than himself, and Ibsen's intense emotional involvement with both, are certainly echoed in *The Master Builder* and *When We Dead Awaken*.

This personal dilemma also sets the outline of the plots, or rather the very marked similarity of the last plots. The resemblance of Solness and Rubek to Ibsen has been commented upon ever since the plays first appeared. But Borkman and Allmers too, with their failed dreams of creativity and their misfitting sexual lives, are thin disguises for Ibsen. And Hilde and Mrs. Solness, Ella Rentheim and her sister Gunhild, Asta and Rita, and (with minor differences) Irene and Maja—the same opposing pair of women—spring straight from Ibsen's life.[4] The fear of death, the sense of artistic failure, or sexual unhappiness and guilty feelings with it—these are the personal aspects of the dramatist's life which certainly underlie the last plays.

But what a profound and rich transformation of the personal do these plays bring into existence! He has succeeded in making his fear of death everyone's fear of death—of the limiting of human hopes and aspirations. He has expressed a direct confrontation of death and human creativity, death and sexuality, that gives the plays a strangely bare and abstract power of their own quite unlike anything else he has written. He has made one of the greatest statements of the relation of the creative side of the artist and the man.

In these plays egotism is the great and characteristic sin. But the egotists—Solness, Allmers, Borkman, and Rubek—are a special variety. They are all seeking to make themselves great in the service of what they regard as an ultimate reality. Solness built churches for God and later "homes for human beings" (Act I, p. 458 and *passim*);[5] Allmers sought to write his great book on human responsibility and then to make his child capable of fulfilling his father's dreams—as no child ever would or could fulfill them; Borkman stole and swindled to liberate "the sleeping spirits of the earth" (Act II, p. 407), to create a world of plenty and happiness; Rubek, the only artist among them labeled as such, made a statue to express the innocence of woman arising after her last sleep, free of contact with earth. The ego which these men aim to gratify is one devoted to the exploration of reality as they understood it, giving shape and form to their findings. They are certainly bent on going up to a high mountain and showing whoever goes with them all the wonders of the world.

But this overwhelming appetite for greatness in disinterested achievement works in its possessor at huge cost and decays into corrupt forms. In the interest of his work or his career he sacrifices lovers, ordinary happiness, even honor and self-respect. Sometimes the sacrifice is direct and crude, exacted at the expense of the loved one. Borkman sold Ella to another man for his bank directorship—and was ruined when the woman did not stand by the bargain. Rubek coldbloodedly saw Irene only as a model for his great statue, and when this purpose was served, "the episode" was over (Act II, p. 484). Sometimes the exploitation is indirect. Then there is victimization of the other one of the recurring pairs of women. Solness, at least at the bar of his own conscience, is guilty of causing the deaths of the little boys and the burning of Aline's house in order to become a successful builder. Allmers had married a woman he did not love in order to have enough money to write his book and to assist the sister he genuinely cared for. In all these instances the result has been the decay and destruction of his own creative life—for which the egotist sacrificed his victims. Nor is the evil of egotism restricted to its possessor. It reaches out to produce in the victims, and especially the women, appalling perversions of true feeling. Gunhild and Rita are horrible examples of possessive jealousy. They are made so, mostly, because they are trying to find fulfillment at a quite unnatural degree of intensity, in their sons or their men, out of frustration of the ordinary relation with a lover.

Yet it cannot be said that the twisted lives of the women, which parallel the self-mutilation of the men, are entirely due to the egotism of the man. It would seem that Ibsen is representing as possible in women also a perverse egotism which is quite native without external justification. Hilde goes on to make Solness *her* Master Builder, at whatever cost to himself—the expression of a power in the world that she longs should exist. In different plays of the middle period, *Rosmersholm* and *Hedda Gabler,* Ibsen has already explored this.

At the moment of the beginning, in each of the four last plays, the man's creative work has been halted or ruined. His happiness, which is the passionate happiness of an artist when his work goes well, has been lost and with it his sense of contact with reality. He connects this loss with his offenses and mistakes against the truth of his own character and inclination. Most frequently the offenses and mistakes are made at the expense of women, both those he loves and sacrifices, and those he sacrifices and does not love. They involve a line of wrong choices between what is "natural" (love, family, children, and ordinary happiness) and what is "artificial" (art and writing and the building of empires). For his guilt and his mistakes he seeks atonement—and the final achievement of his life—in the manner of his death. This is exactly true only of Solness and Rubek, who succeed symbolically in retrieving the losses of their dead period by the resolution of the last venture. Theirs is the true Resurrection. But Allmers and Borkman, even by their failures, tell the same story. Allmers knows that it is his want of passion and his mediocrity that prevent him following Eyolf. Borkman is the dead man who did not awaken, but was put to rest finally in his tomb—because he never understood the mistakes of his earlier egotism but sought to make them over again, because he had not come to terms with the last and final necessary challenge of his life.

It is also only Solness and Rubek who go to their end with true sexual happiness, the one as the willing victim of his lover, the other with his woman as companion. The best that Allmers and Rita can hope for is a dubiously contented partnership in benevolent works, because theirs has never been a genuine love affair anyway; and death and the "icy metal hand" (Act IV, p. 439) have got too secure a grip on Borkman to let him join Ella truly in the encounter with death.

There is in these plays a certain air of extravagance, and something that can most properly be called staginess. The identification of death and the triumph of life, of death and sexual consummation—which is certainly made in both *The Master Builder* and *When We Dead Awaken*—may perhaps be criticized as perverse. But I do not think that this does justice to the peculiar and special subject Ibsen has chosen to express his theme. His *theme* is the appetite for truth and the urge to make something expressive of the truth that is found. But his *subject* is the manifestations of this appetite in men and women who feel it in its most extreme form and therefore are most likely to have it corrupted by egotism, greed, aggressiveness, or self-indulgence. Ibsen is here handling a subject which he deeply understands, the necessary union of the man and the artist and the relation of the two sides of him that make for his creativeness. His tragic vision of this subject is so strong because, rightly or wrongly, in his last days, he felt most intensely the emotion of failure, of failure of creativity. I do not say that Ibsen certainly regarded himself or his work as failures, but he enters into the sense of failure with a strange, bitter avidity, as an actor may do whose potentiality for the expression of despair might be awakened by a mixture of personal and professional causes. The plays, of course, are not representations of *how* the artist fails in his work except glancingly (and not very convincingly) in the account of Rubek's changes in "The Resurrection Day." But what he starts from is the malaise which comes about when the man knows that the spark or creativeness which is the sole outlet for his true experience of reality has given no sign of life for a long time, has perhaps been quenched forever. Now this is an artist's way of seeing the world. The creativeness which is the response to the intense experience of reality is perhaps vestigial in all men. But it is only in the artist that it has this overwhelming compulsiveness so that without it life itself is not worth living. Solness the businessman-builder, Allmers the dilettante, Borkman the industrialist, are all given much more of this passion for creation than they would probably have felt in life—because Ibsen in his own person is nearly incapable of conceiving of life without creation as its end and aim. The sentiment of the artist is all-pervasive in these plays and in all kinds of people, so long as they have any claim to significance for the audience. It is as important as the mark of worth in Brendel, however debased by weakness and charlatanism, as its absence is definitive in Kroll or Tesman.

Ibsen has no belief in the separation of the two sides of the artist's being, his creative personality and his private ordinary life. He thinks that there is a total confluence. The identification of the man and his creative side will inevitably lead to an impossible egotism. The artist who has truly only one object in life, artistic expression, will have to give *his* practice of it, *his* career, *his* work precedence over any ordinary duties, decencies, and kindnesses. This special egotism will eventually load the whole personality with guilt so that there will be no possibility of unself-conscious joy in creation anymore. Ibsen is unquestionably very aware of the kind of victim his sort of artist will make; it may be—I believe it is—true that he thought the process was inevitable, that although the predatory egotism of Solness springs from neurotic fantasy and is extreme of its kind, Rubek, who is no more egotistic than he needs to be in order to be an artist, has also done enough injury to others to ruin his own creative gift and so turn aside to the luxurious life he inwardly despises.

Rosmer says that for the discharge of his task he must have innocence and he must have joy (Act II, p. 303). In these last plays the hero is trying to find both again, having lost both for so long. But the innocence cannot be the virgin innocence of the first statue Rubek tried to make. It must be an innocence that comes of paying the price for past guilt, both as evidence of sincerity and as expiation. It is the test of sincerity as early as *Rosmersholm* between the two lovers, and as a test again in *Little Eyolf* it convicts Allmers and Rita. Because Ibsen accepts no division between the artist and the man and because the artist seems to have been destroyed by the moral defects of the man, he sets about trying to make of life—and necessarily then life's final challenge, death—an image of truth. These deaths—Solness from the top of the tower, Borkman in the snow, Rubek and Irene in the avalanche—are real dramatist's deaths. They show clarity of purpose, courage, and beauty where the rest of the life shows muddle and tawdriness. The dramatist's job (and the actor's) is to invest every detail and gesture of his represented reality with the flavor of significance. When the work is good, it thus re-creates the sensation of the significant discovery which the dramatist himself made in the unordered world of reality outside the theater. But these plays are not even ordinary dramatic re-creations of the ordinary world. (They are indeed hardly dramatic re-creations of the ordinary world at all, in spite of their bourgeois Norwegian setting.) They are the *dramatic* re-creations of the world of a dramatist's fears and hopes. The end of Solness, the end of Rubek, is what Ibsen the *dramatist* hoped for the world, if life itself could be made into a work of art, an image of truth more effective than a play but with all the play's compression and violence. It is not accidental that in Solness' fantasies and in Irene's hallucinations about her experiences Ibsen does not draw the line clearly between what is true and what is not. He is pushing the limits of histrionic art against those of reality, consciously dissolving one into the other.

These deaths are what Ibsen imagined as a "true" artistic image, the resurrection of the artist's creative gift; they are also his resurrection sexually. Particularly in *When We Dead Awaken* is this clear, where the decay of both sides of the man's creativeness, artistic and sexual, is due to the willful surrender, earlier, of what, had he recognized it, should have been most precious to him. Rubek did not want Irene as a woman, only as a model; but when she left him he found that she was the only model that inspired his work. Now although there is an emphasis in this as in the other plays on the sacrifice of what is "natural" for Irene, when she is merely the sculptor's model, and although we are inclined to see this as the typical offense of the one kind of creation at the expense of the other, the matter is apparently not so simple in Ibsen's mind. For both Irene the victim and Rubek the exploiter agree that the satisfaction of ordinary sexual desire would have ruined Rubek's work and Irene's love of him. Their "child," the sculpture, was therefore what the union properly created, that for which Irene willingly made her emotional sacrifice. But the restless egotist in Rubek, who is also the craftsman and who therefore thinks that there must be masterpieces to follow "The Resurrection Day," speaks to Irene of the "episode" (Act II, p. 484) which is finished when the sculpture is completed. It is this which for Irene reduces the uniqueness of the work to the common dimension of one of a line of objects all created to satisfy Rubek's appetite for the expression of reality. So she leaves him, and with her goes Rubek's vision of a pure or idealized version of womanhood. As he continues to work on "The Resurrection Day," the figure recedes into the background as the animal forces of the world come to occupy more and more of the space. When the work is finished, it expresses an imperfect world with aspirations toward something better in it, but not dominating it. With the completion of the sculpture, too, there is an end of Rubek's creative gift, except for a sardonic exploration of the possibilities of the animal faces.

In the new resurrection—death in the high mountains—Rubek and Irene are trying again for the joint re-creation of something both unique and pure, something which Rubek's egotism cannot duplicate and which will undo the meaningless misuse of the intervening years for both the man and the woman. It will be another episode, as Irene grimly reminds Rubek (Act II, p. 488), but this time there will be no recurrence. And this time, the love pact is a genuine partnership which demands sacrifices freely given from both. It is in this sense that death is the final venture of the play, as imaginary and fantastic an expression of sexual creativity as it is of the artistic.

There is a common theme in these four plays rooted in the facts of Ibsen's last years. There is indeed a commonly conceived tragic world which encompasses them all. The characters mean more when their implications are compared than when taken singly. Rubek means more when compared with Solness and Borkman. Ella Rentheim, Irene, and Hilde interact. But of course the plays are not simply the same story with different puppets in the several parts. Ibsen has used the capacity of the theater brilliantly to bring out all the complexity of his subject. Each time he creates a new set of characters who in their particular relation to one another bring that subject to life differently and explore aspects of it that no logical treatment could hope to do. So far I have spoken of what the last plays have in common. Let us now take a closer look at them individually.

The Master Builder

The Master Builder is more full of ambiguities, ultimately perhaps of insoluble riddles, than any of Ibsen's plays. What are we to make of Solness' guilt based on fantasy? Did he burn his house or not? Is he being presented as a near madman—or is the insinuation that there exists a mystical power of mind over matter?[6] What are we to make of the misconceptions between Solness and Aline about their guilt toward one another, and why does Ibsen so conspicuously direct our attention toward them? Most especially, do the ambiguities and doubts rest on the relation of Solness and Hilde? What share does she bear (and how consciously) in the crash from the tower that makes *"My—my* Master Builder!" the appropriate comment? How should we imagine the actress delivering these words most expressively?

The ambiguities are really inherent in the nature of this play. It is not that Ibsen left aspects of the plot which he consciously intended should be read this way or that. Nor, I think, is it that there are relics of personal experience which remain unintegrated and unassimilable, in any ordinary sense. It is rather that although Ibsen was able to generalize his personal experiences (more entirely at the root of this play than any other), the resulting work does not live in the atmosphere of a definite moral judgment. The depth of the experiences enabled him to write this extraordinary love story. Some quality of extended imagination helped him to see a suitable end to it. But the nature of the experience itself, its living force, was too strong and overpowering to conceive the events within a certain moral scheme: to assign a positive value such that Solness was indeed, and not merely in the judgment of most men, "never quite sane on that subject" (Act II, p. 476);[7] to see Hilde as the ironic symbol of the retributive power of youth *or* as the weird evocation of Solness' fantasy and an extension of himself *or* as an innocently devilish young girl who, in ignorance of all the real values of life, spurs her elderly, captivated lover to his death—the last is how Archer wanted to take the story. A satisfactory discussion of the play can hardly hope to establish more definitely the meaning of such things as the catastrophe. It can only consider more of the colors and shadows that lie on the persons and the action.

Retribution is in the air in *The Master Builder,* from beginning to end. Solness is afraid of retribution, afraid that youth will come knocking at the door and call an end to the success of the Master Builder. He is so afraid of retribution that he hopes to liquidate some of its power, inherent in his guilt toward his wife, by allowing Aline to suspect him unjustly with Kaja Fosli. He is afraid of the Broviks, despite their very limited gifts. And not only is the fear of retribution in the air of the play. It is in its structure. At the simplest level, Hilde is the retributive agent who will do to Solness what he has done to others—make him an instrument for the achievement of her desires and fantasies. And it may be that even Solness' peculiar God, who is thought of as having taken away his children in order to make him work harder as a church builder, is conceived of as a force of retribution, striking down the presumptuous man who aspired to be a creator equal with himself.

In regard to Hilde and Solness the dialogue in Act III is crucial. To me it seems certain that Solness hypnotizes Hilde, as, we are told, he had already done to Kaja Fosli—or at least he concentrates on Hilde the dominating power of his will as he had done in the other instance, if hypnotism is too technical a word for the process. In his earlier conversation with Herdal, where Solness is telling what happened between him and Kaja he says, "I just stood looking at her" (Act I, p. 444), and later the girl acted as though they had made a verbal agreement by which Kaja would work in his office on his own terms. In the scene in Act III (p. 496) the stage directions say: "Solness lets his eyes dwell on her." She answers "as though half-asleep." This is twice repeated ("Hilde, as before"). She appears to answer from a kind of trance. With the recollection of the former story of Kaja in mind, the reader, and spectator, is ready for her surrender to Solness' influence. At this stage Solness is supposed to be trying to keep Hilde with him against her will. She has determined to leave him after the conversation with Aline. Injuring someone you know is a different thing from doing wrong to a stranger, and Hilde's theoretically "robust" conscience is not robust enough to help her through this experience. Solness is trying hard to influence her. He uses her own words against her, "the robust conscience" and the "bird of prey," and now all her answers come in this trance-like state. Suddenly the stage directions read: "Hilde sits erect on the bench, once more full of animation. Her eyes are happy and sparkling." What follows in the dialogue is all important, for we expect that Solness has mastered her will—and indeed he has. We hear no more of any assaults of conscience, and she stays. But the result is different from that of the incident with Kaja. For there Solness knew exactly what he wanted his victim to do and the victim obliged. Now what he wants is still obscure even to himself and only becomes clear to him through the mouth of this girl. It is she who now determines the course of action. It is *my* kingdom and *my* castle that he must build, and when he eventually falls he is *my* Master Builder. Yet the effect is not totally that of the magician's genie which he cannot control and which works his destruction. This is indeed the simple impression but not that left by a more thoughtful reading or representation. Her plan is an emanation of his will as well as hers. He finds in it a revelation of new possibilities as a human being and an artist. He is the one who adds the significant words "on a firm foundation" after "castles-in-the-air" (Act III, p. 498), and I am almost sure that they mean his own death, the only sure foundation for the extreme preservation of the dreams, free of the destructive power of time and change. If this interpretation is right, Solness does, effectively, will his own death, and finds the end he chooses.

But he does so through an intermediary. He tells us earlier that according to his own theory the "troll in him" (Act II, p. 481)—his brutal, selfish egotism—calls to his aid the helpers and servers. These are apparently later referred to as the "blond devils and dark devils" and, apparently again, the fair-haired are good and the dark-haired bad ("Good devils and bad devils. Blond devils and dark devils! If only we could be sure which kind had hold of us" [Act II, p. 481]). I believe that Hilde is one of the fair-haired kind, that Solness' troll has summoned to him, and that in the end the death she brings him is what he wishes would happen.

But what he wants then, is very different from anything he has "wanted" in that sense before. It involves a surrender to the power which not only serves but also guides him, and is a kind of self-sacrifice which is the very antithesis of the trollishness that summoned her originally. He is moving, at last clear of doubt and the haunting of guilt, real and imaginary, to his meeting with destiny as surely as Peer goes to meet the Button Moulder at the turn of the road. This is the sense in which the events at Lysanger ten years before become really important. For, in the first place, in main outline they undeniably happened—unlike the murky chain of causation involved in the burning of the house or the origin of Aline's unhappiness—and, equally undeniably, that day, for his own purposes, Solness climbed the tower he had built. Second, the Lysanger episode in all its detail is a dress rehearsal for the last scene of the play.

Solness' career as a builder had three phases. In the first he built churches with towers; in the second he built homes for happy human beings—with the determination that for himself at least one home should have a tower reaching upward; in the third he sought to make his "castles-in-the-air with a firm foundation" which is the "one possible dwelling place for human happiness" (Act III, p. 505). The division between his first and second phases was marked by the climbing of the tower at Lysanger, between the second and the third by the climbing of the tower over his own home. When he climbed the tower at Lysanger he formally resigned from the service of his jealous Lord because he had resolved to be a creator as free in his sphere as the Deity. To assert his right and validate it into existence he performed the "impossible," the conquest of his terror of giddiness, of falling from the pinnacle. But the theory of his second phase as craftsman was mistaken. There is no use for "happy homes" for human beings because there is no happiness to be found in this way, according to Solness. This leads him to the new resolve that he will build "the loveliest thing in the world" (Act III, p. 498), which is castles-in-the-air. When Hilde scornfully links their airiness to his "dizzy conscience," he adds quietly, "on a firm foundation." The new element added to the fantastic structure to take care of the dizzy conscience, and to preserve the dream, will be his death. He will validate his right as a free creator again by performing the impossible. He will mount the tower and converse with the Lord God as an equal—and then he will "come down" and embrace his princess—and pay for his dizzy conscience. For "the little devil in white" (Act I, p. 453) that had so scared him at Lysanger ten years ago when she shouted hurrah at he stood on the height will cry again this time, and this time it will be the signal for the payment.

Thus the feeling of the play indicates that the presence of the girl at the two critical moments of Solness' life is a fact of destiny —a dramatist's destiny of course. The association with her will be the objective factor in setting him on his right course to its appropriate end. Hilde is the one he is "almost sure" he must have summoned to himself (Act II, p. 483). She is "that Youth" whom he is so afraid of and toward whom in his heart he yearns so deeply.

Through the play there is a steady revolution in his relations with Hilde. When she tells him of the events in Lysanger—with the detail of the kiss and the promised kingdom (Act I, pp. 452–56)—his first impulse is to deny that they happened. The second is to see in this one more example of the inexplicable power of his imagination. He had *wanted* these things to happen, had wanted to kiss the little girl and promise to carry her off to her kingdom in ten years' time, and so, because his thoughts and wishes seem to have the capacity of turning fantasy into reality, Hilde had believed in the kiss and the promise as actual events.

But the common dreams of falling shared by both of them, the coincidence of her thought and his that he, Solness, is "the only one who should be allowed to build" (Act II, p. 470) make him wonder about the nature of the relationship. He is beginning to see Hilde no longer as a possible victim of his powers of imagination but, with pleasure, as an extension of himself in the directions he would prefer—toward boldness, resolution, generosity. She is in fact becoming his "better" self. Under her influence, though with some misgivings, he can afford to abandon his fears of the Broviks and his cowardly selfishness toward Kaja. Yet this domination by the new influence is a strange thing, for it steadily becomes on his part a voluntary surrender made to the being that demands it—but he knows far better than she what a sacrifice she is calling for. The castle will have "a tremendously high tower."

SOLNESS (*softly*): Will the Master Builder be allowed to come up to the princess?

HILDE: If the Master Builder will.

SOLNESS (*more softly still*): Then I think he will come.

HILDE (*nods*): Yes. The Master Builder will come.

SOLNESS: But he'll never build any more—poor Master Builder!

[Act III, p. 497]

Solness is looking for an appropriate end for himself, a consummation to life as immense and significant as he had wanted his life to be—and as it had not been, despite its apparent success. The coming of Hilde into his life had suggested the renewal of the hopes of greatness and of aspiration. She seems indeed to have been called to help him. But, as in *When We Dead Awaken,* the revival of hope and the last chance have come to a relatively old man. The hope and the chance must bear on the old man's natural foe, death, and its natural challenge. The hope and the chance call for the sacrifice of most of the days that are left, in order to invest the last struggle with meaning. Before the conversation in which Solness tries to induce Hilde to stay with him against her conscience, he had seen the revival of his youth in a love affair. But she did not want that man, the human lover, but the idol of her fantasy, who could climb as high as he built, as flawless humanly, as free of weakness, as the limitless heights of excitement suggested by his tower. Suddenly he realizes that to be this idol if only for a moment, and especially if that moment were to end in death, was his life's proper conclusion. To be that idol for the moment meant to overcome his greatest weakness, the fear of falling. Even when he was younger it had been with him, always. It is years now since he has tried to deal with it. But "the impossible" beckons. If he can achieve it, he has become "*my* Master Builder"—and he has fulfilled all his dreams in the consummation of a moment. Death is both the price and the security, for after this one test there will be no more. The castle will have been built with a firm foundation under it, for it will be no longer necessary to reconcile it with reality.

In this play the emphasis on Solness' powers of imagination, the ability of his mind to translate wish into fact, is unique in Ibsen, except for a shadowy repetition in *Little Eyolf*. A great deal of space and dramatic interest is given to this, which makes one speculate on just how he meant the two parts of his play to be related—Solness' strange gifts and the pre-Hilde piece of his career, and Solness' willing death at Hilde's hands.

When Solness tells his story to Hilde he asks the same question as he asked Dr. Herdal (Act I, p. 446)—in effect, Am I mad? She answers that there is nothing the matter with his intellect, only with his conscience (Act II, p. 480). It is his sense of guilt that maims him, and keeps him afraid. He cannot face the implications of being as great as it is within his capacity to be, for this means the readiness to sacrifice others, or use them.

So far Hilde's explanation; and as far as it goes, it is true enough, for the two characters concerned. But Ibsen knows another side of this and he knows the special meaning and depth of the neurosis he attributes to Solness. He has explained the meaning more fully, I believe, in *When We Dead Awaken,* in the dialogue between Rubek, Ulfhejm, and Maja.

> ULFHEJM [to Maja]: . . . Your husband and I both work in hard material, Madame. He struggles with great blocks of marble, I presume; and I struggle with the quivering sinews of the bear. And in the end we conquer—both of us. In spite of its resistance, we master our material and vanquish it. . . . Yes, I'm sure marble puts up a good fight too. It's dead, and it resents being hammered into life. And when you try to prod a bear out of his lair—he resents it too!
>
> [Act I, p. 455]

Solness is the man whose mind has presented him with a distorted picture of himself as an artist in life, where the material willingly follows his impulse and plastically takes on the impress of his will. None of the things he achieves has any value, but the guilt of having brought them about, at the necessary cost to others, is still with him. The struggle with the stone, and with the bear's sinews, is the necessary condition of significant success, and even meaning.

This is where the climbing of the tower comes in. The conquest of this psychological and physical difficulty, so immediate and palpable, is the antidote to his fantasy that everything physical and mental automatically obeys his will. This needs a powerful struggle and it also implies death when the struggle is over. This means to be confronted with the undeniable ultimate—and with the achievement of his dream at the same time. If he can climb the towered house, with the spire pointing heavenward like a church, he is the true artist, the artist in life who can climb as high as he builds. He is indeed a creator as free as God, as he expresses it himself (Act III, p. 505).

But the play is a play about a love affair, as we are told Ibsen said himself.[8] And there are two parties to this love affair—Hilde as well as Solness. Hilde is personally responsible for Solness' death, and the fact that she pronounces the valediction on herself and Solness, in the last words of the play, emphasizes the dramatist's concern with her. Hilde's cry, "Hurrah for Master Builder Solness," certainly is the signal for his fall, and there is very little doubt that it causes the fall. We are told by Solness himself that at Lysanger ten years before he had "nearly" fallen when one of those little devils in white had shouted hurrah, and Herdal and Aline had been constantly urging everyone to keep quiet as soon as they have identified the mounting figure as that of Solness. If then Hilde, consciously or otherwise, kills him, what does Ibsen want us to make of it?

There is something curious about the responsibility for the hero's death in several of the last plays, although in none of the others can it be so clearly laid at the door of the woman he loved as this one. Both Borkman and Rubek are, in Ibsen's terms, indirectly assassinated by their rejected and now resurrected loves. Ella Rentheim denounces Borkman, "I prophesy . . . you will never enter in triumph into your cold, dark, kingdom" (Act IV, p. 438), and the prophecy has the quality of a sentence of death, which in fact it proves to be. It is Irene who proposes the night on the upland which is to be the scene of the death of Rubek and herself. We should perhaps see Hilde's action in the context of the others. In all three cases it seems that the woman's action is calculated to preserve the integrity of her dream pattern of the man's character, the image of the hero, at the expense of his life.

But not only is Hilde directly the cause of the fall—her attitude after it is remarkable in the extreme. All the more so, because it puts her "robust" conscience to its fullest test, and when subjected earlier to another contact with reality it was not so very robust. Hilde believed herself the bird of prey until she saw Aline Solness as the victim. Then the role of the predator was too uncomfortable to sustain (Act III, pp. 490–94). But there is a difference, and perhaps it is important, that in the original conversation with Solness she had defended her claim to a robust conscience on the grounds that she had been willing to abandon the father she had loved and would never see again (Act II, p. 481). Hilde's robust conscience would not support her in ruining the lives of miserable secondary victims in whom she felt no interest. But she was sufficiently ruthless to herself and anyone she loved. This love must find its expression in action and trial. It lived completely only in passionate expression. Since the conversation in which she realized that the climbing of the tower was the only means by which her hero would achieve his perfection, there is nothing on her mind but anticipation of that moment. It is a moment of victory and she enjoys it. What happened afterward is of no consequence and she ignores it. He has won.

> HILDE (*turns to* RAGNAR *and says quietly*): I can't see him up there any more.
> RAGNAR: What a ghastly thing. So—after all—he couldn't do it.
> HILDE (*as though under a spell, with a quiet triumph*): But he climbed to the very top. And I heard harps in the air. (*Waves the shawl and cries out with wild intensity*) My—my Master Builder!
>
> [Act III, p. 510]

There is certainly a total alienation from ordinary human feelings in this, but it may be that this is the last evidence of Solness' magical gift applied to her. This is the way he would have her think. Whatever the future might be for a hypothetical Hilde living beyond the limits of the play—madness or just disintegration—everything important in the world ended with the sound of harps in the air. They are a strange pair of lovers, but perhaps in the last act they found their innocence and joy.

Little Eyolf

Little Eyolf, the second play of the "series," has close relation-
ships to both *The Master Builder,* which directly preceded it, and
Rosmersholm. The play is about responsibility and its meaning.
Its subject is a murder—as definitely as in *Rosmersholm* though
it is wishes, rather than suggestion, that cause it. The magical
activity of the wish links *Eyolf* with *Master Builder.* The re-
morseless investigation of guilt follows in the track of the real
wishes and intentions of the participants, and this exploration is
far more thoroughgoing than in *Master Builder.*

That the play is about a murder is not obvious at first reading,
except in the sense that the death of the little boy is brought about
by the dubious activities of the Rat-Woman.[9] The rational account might indeed, truthfully, be that given by Allmers—though
immediately rejected by him. But the truthfulness of the rational
account of what happened has no more to do with the real facts
than the first accounts of Beata's death have to do with what happened at Rosmersholm. The world does *not* run so at haphazard,
at least not this world of Ibsen's dramatic fantasy. For when they
dig deeper—Allmers and Rita, and Allmers and Asta—they find
an explanation that is far more convincing and far more horrible.
It is Rita's wish that strikes down the child, because he is spir-
itually the true child of Asta and Allmers. His aunt has always
stood like a wall between him and his natural mother. Rita has
felt him to be not a link with her husband, but a competitor for
his love.

But she has not ever admitted to anyone, perhaps not to herself, that she wanted to kill him because of his relationship to
Asta and Allmers in conjunction. *That* we only understand very
late, when at the scene by the fjord Asta presents Allmers with
the water lilies from both of the Eyolfs, the big and the little.

Not the least of the brilliance of this play is that it discloses the full significance of the plot only piece by piece. In the end only Allmers and the audience possess a complete picture of what happened and all the interacting motives.

There are two elements whose conjunction ensures Eyolf's death —the Rat-Woman and Rita's hatred. We get them in this order. The threat of the Rat-Woman hangs over Eyolf but it is the force of Rita's hatred which consigns him to the class of victims unwanted, worrying, and therefore subject to the Rat-Woman's deadly pity. All we have in the scene between her and the inhabitants of the house is the sense of the impending relationship of the boy and the old woman. Eyolf is first horrified and then fascinated by Pug-boy just as the rats are.

RAT-WOMAN: Come along, young master! Have you ever seen such a sweet, lovable face? . . .

EYOLF (*in an undertone, staring fixedly at the dog*): I think he has the ugliest, most awful face I've ever seen.

RAT-WOMAN (*closing the bag*): It'll come—you'll see—it'll come.

EYOLF (*drawing nearer in spite of himself; then he goes right up to the bag and strokes it*): Still—he *is* lovely. He's lovely all the same.

[Act I, p. 309]

In the first serious conversation between Allmers and his wife one is apt to be overpowered by the sense of her obsessive jealousy, her unwillingness to share his love with any human being. As usual, Ibsen is using the violence of her passion to make us look closer at its origin. Allmers is bored with Rita, and also feels guilty toward her. Her jealousy and desperation are largely due to an understanding that his attitude toward her misery is one of detachment. The book and the child, first the one and then the other, are her rivals for his interest. The book is identified as being his and Asta's joint product. We only gradually understand that the child is even more so. Rita is unfeignedly glad that he has given up the book. She is now bent on getting rid of the child. As they discuss the unhappy little being's deficiencies, it transpires almost accidentally that his crippling is due to a fall from a table, on the occasion when Allmers, with guilty cruelty, had just told his wife of the seeming innocence of his relation to Asta which resulted in both sister and son bearing the same name. Rita seduces Allmers into the moment of forgetfulness when the child fell and was maimed. From this moment his aunt tries to take him away from Rita. She instinctively feels the threat of ultimate destruction hanging over the boy. When Allmers decides to give up the book, and concentrate on his son's future, on equipping the boy with "a sense of happiness," Rita, again balked of the love she wanted from Allmers, wishes him dead. And the Rat-Woman executes her wishes.

Rita and Allmers, then, are guilty of the death of Eyolf: the woman, because she brought it about—no more in this play than in *The Master Builder* does Ibsen clearly indicate the nature of this magical power; the man, because it is his wrong to Rita that made her act as she has. (The two have a curiously close relationship to Rosmer and Rebekka in this respect.) Through the tortured obscurities of motive Allmers tries to find his way to a definition of the sense of responsibility about which he had ineffectively written. Ibsen's irony here is cruel enough. Allmers abandons his book on human responsibility after his encounter with death on the mountain because he feels, like all the heroes of Ibsen's last series, that art is a poor second to life, and so he turns from writing to the raising of the child—and the provision for him of conscious happiness! When the child drowns, Allmers not only discovers much about human responsibility that would never have been in his book; it becomes clear that the boy himself has never existed distinctly for either Allmers or his wife. He was merely the object of the woman's hatred and the man's twisted fantasy. Between the two mental constructions all that is left of the living boy is swept out to sea. Only the crutch is floating, the symbol of guilt which exists after he is gone, to reveal the truth to his parents about each other. The discovery of truth comes about through the sting of conscience, and remorse stimulates the appetite for reality that will satisfy the sense of retribution. Here Allmers shows a purpose and relentlessness which he has shown nowhere else. Death is real enough. "Supposing you could follow Eyolf; . . . Supposing you were absolutely sure of finding him again? Of knowing him, and understanding him—? . . . Would you be willing—quite deliberately—to follow him?" he asks Rita.

"No."

"But supposing *I* were to go to Eyolf. . . . Then would you come?"

". . . Yes! I'd want to! But— . . . No—I'm sure I couldn't" (Act II, pp. 341–42). Allmers, as well as Rita is "earthbound," and some token of retribution paid is the nearest the two of them will come to a living gesture that expresses reality. So the boys of the village will be put in Eyolf's place by Rita to fill the vacant space with something like love, and perhaps Allmers, between the dead-and-the-lost and the living shadow of love expresses himself not unfitly in the feeble sentimentality of the last lines.

In general Allmers is weak and mediocre. At times his dishonesty leads him into positive perversity as when he supports Rita's plea to Asta to stay with them, with *both of them,* and "share our life" (Act III, p. 355). But Ibsen expresses through Allmers, and sympathetically, one notion which is very important in these last plays, which looks backward to Solness' last moment and forward to Rubek and Irene. This is the "Law of Change." Allmers admits that his love, like his life itself, will always be subject to the law of change—except for the love of brother and sister, because that is holy and taboo (Act II, p. 346). His love for Asta was nourished by its intense artificiality: it could absorb shocks without self-conscious examination because the *assumption* was that the love of brother for sister would always be the same.

Even when he knows that they are no longer so related Allmers wishes blindly to pretend that they are. That is because he is both weak and dishonest. But there is in Ibsen's mind a supreme value associated with the notions of uniqueness and unchange-ability. It is the true holy place. When life, in its ordinary course, negates it, it is unsatisfactory. When art exploits the sentiment and makes a trade of its creation, it is bad. Life, with the quality of art, in its singleness and intensity, is what he is looking for. He explores his despair once more in Borkman, before he finds the image of hope in *When We Dead Awaken*.

John Gabriel Borkman

Borkman is different from both Solness and Rubek, in that the dramatist has chosen another aspect of the despair of failure. Solness and Rubek had, in their ways, had success, and the taste of it had turned bitter and meaningless. But Borkman is, as he says himself, a Napoleon "shot and maimed in his first battle" (Act II, p. 395). The sense of frustration is almost unbearable, for this man has not had the chance to make his mistakes to the point at which he would be weary of them. Had he done so, had Hinkel not "betrayed" him, we would have had a figure like Solness and Rubek—for like them Borkman is a man who will sacrifice what is nearest and dearest to him in pursuit of his dreams, and will later find that he has ruined the creative gift for which he made the sacrifice. But the special emphasis in this play is that Borkman does not in fact know what he could have done, even by the world's estimation. He is dying of want of self-confidence only very slightly masked by his arrogance.

Throughout the play he is in his death agony. He is neither as Gunhild with outrageous cruelty suggests, already dead when she bids him, "Stay buried in your grave" (Act III, p. 418), nor like Solness and Rubek, possessed of life energy intact though sleeping. He lives, if one can call it life, between a desperate belief in the value of opportunity—and an equally desperate hope that as an "exceptional" man he is above the accidental event. He is a man ruined beyond revival, but never admitting it, falsifying or remaking the past because there is no future and really no present. Gunhild, immobile and watching down below in that house of watching and waiting, hears him come down again and again, take his coat and hat, move to go out, only to abandon the effort again and retire upstairs (Act I, pp. 374–75). "The pacing of the wolf" haunts the first half of the play.

Borkman makes a more naked statement of his obsession than any of the other heroes of the series. It is quite simply the will to possess infinite power. Of course he speaks of this in philanthropic terms. He talks of the thousands of industries that would have arisen at the touch of his magic wand and the thousands of workers that would have been made happy by him. But what spurs him on is really different from all this. It is the singing of the spirits of the mine. "You begged to be liberated and I tried to free you. . . . I love you, as you lie there, dormant, buried in the darkness! I love you, unborn forces yearning for the light! I love you with all your dazzling train of power and glory! I love you, love you, love you!" (Act IV, p. 438).[10] The power to give happiness to others, especially anonymous thousands of others, is just one aspect of the deliciousness of power. It is certainly not the heart of the attraction.

For John Gabriel has destroyed his one hope of resurrection, as Solness and Rubek had never completely done. Ella says: "You have been twice guilty of murder. You've not only killed my soul—you've killed your own as well" (Act II, p. 407). The murder of the soul is the murder of the love life in a human being. Borkman does not get the chance to build his empire, and the guilt of the murder remains. He has also begun to realize that the destruction of the human part of him, which craved the companionship of another, to share, love, and create, would have allowed him neither happiness nor contentment, even had he carried out his plans successfully. At the end of his life Ibsen is insistent on this one element in his tragic theme—there can be no success built on the surrender of a man's deepest sexual attachment. The kingdom and the power and the glory are not only a poor bargain for the loss. They do not come into your possession—only their mirage.

What is terrible in Borkman is that there is in him no capacity for a last effort. It is true that his entry into the world of snow and pines with Ella reminds us of the last moments of Rubek and Irene. But Borkman is still possessed by the old ambitions. There *is* no chance of their fulfillment, but, if there were, one might still feel with Ella, as he lies dead on the snow. "It's best so, John Gabriel; best—for you" (Act IV, p. 439).

In *Borkman* as in *When We Dead Awaken* there is a contrast between the agonized struggle for the renewal of life and the simpler and more ordinary effort toward a more ordinary happiness. In *Borkman* the latter is expressed by Erhart and his marriage with Fanny Wilton. There are curious overtones to the contrast. The neglect of human happiness implied in Borkman's egotism is hateful. But there is something sardonic in Ibsen's representation of the simpler approaches to happiness. Little Frida is being taken along by Fanny Wilton against the day when either she or Erhart get tired of each other's company. And in *When We Dead Awaken*, Maja does not find her bear hunter all that she wanted him to be. Though Borkman, Ella, and Gunhild are all people in their death throes, they have more sense of life and its meaning than Erhart and Fanny. The latter are young and perhaps, Ibsen implies, they are right. Erhart cannot spare two months to his dying foster mother, but then perhaps those two months are all the opportunity he has. Ibsen is skeptical of the conjunction of man and his opportunity. You had better seize it when you get the chance. So Foldal is run over by the sleigh and Ella must die alone and Gunhild wither away and John Gabriel perish loneliest of all. Maybe, as Ella says, there *is* happiness for Erhart. But in any case he is young and is doing just what is expected of him, and is natural for him to do. But Erhart Borkman will never be a man like his father either, an "exceptional" man, and Fanny is neither Ella nor Gunhild. In these plays the sympathy is only for the exceptional man or woman, even in failure. For out of their failure there was for Ibsen the only kind of success that counted, albeit a renewal, a second chance, only.

When We Dead Awaken

The last play, *When We Dead Awaken,* is pre-eminently a play of mood. The action is vestigial. It consists merely of the meeting of Irene and Rubek at the sanitarium and the departure to the mountain resort of the two couples, Maja and Ulfhejm, Rubek and Irene. There is a sort of formal break between Rubek and Maja which splits the four into their natural pairs. The rest is only the scene on the mountainside when Maja and Ulfhejm go back and Rubek and Irene go on to meet their death in the avalanche. There are almost no minor characters, unless Ulfhejm is considered as such. The Inspector and the Deaconess are in the nature of lay figures. Apparently Ibsen had some notion of including certain other characters but abandoned it.

The play has never been popular and is now hardly ever performed. From the first, William Archer, Ibsen's lifelong friend and English translator, regarded it as almost a "pathological" work, and he seems to think that Ibsen's breakdown which followed the completion of the play is already showing signs of its presence.[11]

Yet nowhere, almost, on the stage of western Europe is there a play which has transformed into an appropriate dramatic expression such inward and personal reflections. Nowhere without the aid of poetry has such solidity been given to the mood of despair and ultimately the mood of victory, rendered only by conversations between two people, mostly dealing with actions of the past.

The play is a play of mood and the mood is the mood of a moment—the last moment of a life and how it should be lived. As Rubek asks, "What do we really see?" when we dead awaken, and Irene's answer is, "that we have never lived" (Act III, p. 489). The conclusion is the struggle to make of this last moment, before they go down to death again for the second and final time, something of glory and significance.

Ibsen had previously treated the notion of a metaphorical death and its relation to the real thing. Borkman is, according to Gunhild, dead already; he should "stay buried" in his grave (Act III, p. 418). It is easy to criticize and say that this is an outworn metaphor meaning little more than that life is dull and meaningless. But Ibsen does more than that with the image, particularly in *When We Dead Awaken*. Indeed his whole use of images in this play is especially effective. The dull little railway station at night, the train stopped for no reason, the two men walking up and down engaging in "totally unnecessary conversation" (Act I, pp. 445–46); the extraordinary confusion in Irene's distorted mind between the strait jacket and the coffin (Act I, pp. 460–61); the figure of the black-robed Deaconess—nurse—

shadow—jailer—omen of death? Ibsen keeps us at exactly the right level of imagery, between the tangible and the fantastic. The whole of the early part of the play is concerned with the sense of flatness and gloom that is now Rubek's life. There he sits in the meaningless luxury of the sanitarium with four to five years of life behind when he has never really done a day's work with vigor and enjoyment—ever since "The Resurrection Day" finally went out into the world: opposite him the girl whom he has bought along with the villa at Taunitz and its furniture; the sense of the intolerableness of it all mounting in him, with no relief except to move from place to place, from the resort hotel to the sea voyage and back to Germany. This is the moment "when we dead awaken." That moment and the possibility that anything different could lie beyond it is bound up with the interpretation of the occasion when his invention and creativity ceased, and when he lost the woman who had stimulated them.

The appearance of Irene starts his speculations on the value of the statue, what happened to it and why she left him. And this is the turning point of the piece. It is the beginning of the awakening. Irene says, "But now—I'm just beginning to rise again from the dead" (Act I, p. 461). She later declares that taking Rubek for alive she found her mistake. He had been dead like herself. And so what they can do is only "play" because, "There can be no resurrection for the life we had together" (Act II, p. 486). But in the end Rubek realizes and convinces her that there can be one more venture which will reassert life, and will moreover reassert it in the sense that originally the statue, "The Resurrection Day," had done. Thus "The Resurrection Day"— what is meant as a work of art, what this implies about life, and how this meaning can at last be expressed not in art but in life itself—that is the theme of the play.

Rubek makes two statements about the statue's subject. "I wanted to create the image of a pure young woman, awakening

on Resurrection Day. Nothing in that higher, freer, happier region would seem strange to her—or new, or different. While on
earth she had known only joy, and purity, and innocence; and,
on awakening from the long sleep of death, she finds herself
unchanged" (Act I, p. 463). Later in a more difficult passage he
describes the statue (or rather its original design) as "a beautiful,
virginal young woman. . . . Her life on this earth had left her
pure and untouched as a child; and when she awoke in the
glorious light, she had no evil to atone for" (Act II, p. 481).

Perhaps the most revealing description comes from Irene herself, who, in telling how she went with Rubek on their strange
pilgrimage, says, "That was my resurrection. I awoke from the
deep slumber of childhood—and followed you" (Act I, p. 462).
We will do well to remember the phrase in *Rosmersholm,* "Innocence, yes. Happiness and joy cannot exist without it" (Act IV,
p. 332).

What happened to the statue when Irene went away? She left
Rubek because he had spoken of their joint work on the statue
as an "episode" (Act II, p. 484) and because he clearly thought
that the statue was unique only in the way any work of his was
unique but that he would naturally go on to do others. This was
from Irene's point of view sheer blasphemy. She had thought
of the work with exactly the wholehearted devotion of the
mother to her child. She had thought of this as hers and Rubek's
child. Suddenly to see it as a work in a series of works all created
to gratify Rubek's restless appetite for the expression of reality
was more than she would tolerate. Irene was under the impression that the statue was finished when she and Rubek parted.

What follows is one of the strangest things in the play. Rubek
apparently kept working over the piece and tried to accommo-
date its design to his changing sense of reality. Archer denounces
this as a total impossibility. It is one of the counts on which he
condemned Ibsen's craftsmanship in the last play. "In conceiving
it," he says, "we are deserting the domain of reality and plunging

into some fourth dimension where the properties of matter are other than those we know."[12] I do not know why Archer was so vehement in his comment. It is clearly not so impossible as all this. It is admittedly unlikely that a sculptor would take years over a group and change the design as he spent time on it—but it is not impossible. What Rubek apparently did was to make three changes. One, the position of the central figure was moved back and was now surrounded by animal faces; second, the expression of the face itself was changed, which meant that in fact he remade the whole of the head; and third, he included the figure of the tortured man in the foreground (Act II, pp. 481–82). On the whole, it sounds to us like a very bad bit of sculpture, but it is not Ibsen's judgment of sculpture we are concerned with, nor his romantic conception of what it can "mean." For what Ibsen really meant to say has little to do with sculpture and everything to do with writing and his own life. Rubek feels tortured because he has lost his vision of the world and has been forced to see it tenanted by animal faces. Ibsen is an artist who has to go on writing but in his writing must take account of his change of position. Of course, as a writer, he can change his subject and the special work on which he is engaged, finish one and start another. But his feeling of the continuity is so strong that he chooses to express this as the experience of a sculptor who works on the same statue all the time, changing it as he himself changes in his understanding of life. I think it may well be that Ibsen's self-proclaimed single design for his last four plays has something to do with this. "The series which ended with the Epilogue really started with *Master Builder*." In this unified work, I believe, he was trying, as Rubek was, to make a reconciliation between his earlier vision and the animal faces. And I believe that the conflicting demands centered in sexual happiness and love. And so, rather inevitably, the tendency is to elevate the claims of life, of human happiness, over those of the artist with what now appears to Ibsen to be his *essentially* perverse passion to represent and explain everything instead of actually living. But all the same, this notion of life is for Ibsen an illusion. In fact what he wants is life as a kind of artifact to supersede the artifact of the book. It is of a play that he is thinking. The man in the foreground of the sculpture is denounced by Irene as full of self-pity and as a "poet" (Act II, p. 483). Ibsen wanted to be just that "poet," in a composition which was *real;* he wanted to feel the expiation of his guilt (whatever it may have consisted in), and the moment of grandeur in his death, which he knew was near. Since the only way to achieve these ends was to represent them in a play, the play itself had to take account of the two levels. One of these, the sculpture, stood for Ibsen's past "mistakes" or what now appeared mistakes; the other, confronting death with his loved one on the mountainside, stood for the resurrection of his power. This power was the power to see the vision of purity and ordinariness ("nothing . . . would seem strange to her—or new, or different" [Act I, p. 463]) triumphing over the animal forces which at times seemed to him to dominate the world and reduce everything to a Dead Sea of dullness and insignificance.

In this histrionic rendering of the theme of art versus life, Maja and Ulfhejm have their place. Ibsen has pointed to the resemblance of Rubek and the bear hunter in the passage already quoted. "Your husband and I both work in hard material . . ." (Act I, p. 455). Later Maja, in her conversation with Rubek about her preference for Ulfhejm says, "He's not a bit of an artist," and Rubek smiling answers, "I'm sure you're right in that" (Act II, p. 468). Ibsen is trying to establish something here in this sequence of curiously contradictory statements. The work of the artist and this man who wrests some meaning from life, to his own joy and danger, are, in a sense alike. Both are incessantly struggling to an objective which is elusive; both are working with material which is recalcitrant. But as Maja sees him, and Rubek, too, with his relatively slight interest in Ulfhejm's personality, the bear hunter is direct, simple, uncomplicated in his pursuit of his end, with presumably no sense of bad conscience or missed opportunities which attend the artist. This may be the view of him, as seen by Maja and Rubek, but we may reasonably doubt whether the dramatist's authority goes with it. In an unguarded moment in the last act, in conversation with Maja, the fierce, innocent Ulfhejm reveals himself as the tortured cuckold to whom hunting, of animals or women, is the only release from the sense of failure and to whom the mountains are the only refuge from the uncleanness of the world.

Maja's enthusiasm for freedom seems simple enough. There is an agreeable want of reaction to Rubek's cruelty when he tells her of his indifference to her, his boredom with their joint life. (This is a brilliantly rendered conversation, because all of Rubek is there, his subtlety and perception of human feelings giving way before the onset of his desire to be finished and done with the death in life the two had experienced.) Maja indeed seems to be able to deal with Rubek remarkably well, and he is clearly taken somewhat aback at her lack of any resentment, or interest almost, at his announcement. She is as ready to part from him as he from her. She is sure that in the bear hunter she has found the excitement which Rubek has promised and never delivered. He had taken her up to the high mountain but had not shown her all the glory of the world. But the last of Maja is no more hopeful than the first, as far as her happiness is concerned. She is no more at home in the discomfort of the physical mountains with her savage lover than she was on Rubek's metaphysical heights. The truth is, as Rubek brutally puts it, "Somehow I don't think you were made for mountain climbing, little Maja" (Act I, p. 449). There is no easy way to the enterprise which will express your sense of reality, no childish simplicity of acceptance and effort. You must have innocence and joy, but the innocence must be bred of payment for past guilt and understanding of its meaning. The joy must come from some deep region of man's consciousness which is never devoid of suffering.

In no figure has Ibsen been able to dramatize more effectively the combination of despair and hope than in Irene. She is perhaps the very greatest of his heroines. Lunacies included, she represents in an extraordinary but quite credible way the *resurrection* of the personality, mutilated, but lying awaiting the call to life. In her accounts of herself there is a marvellous shading from the indisputably proved horror to the horrors that are purely fantastic and that leave one with all the greater fear because they cannot be pinned down to a certain meaning. Granted the suicide of her first husband, what of the "turntable" that showed her naked to the gaze of everyone? What of the "deaths" or "murders" of the children? What of, "Then they lowered me into a tomb. There were bars at the window and padded walls; so that the shrieks from the tomb might not disturb those in the world above" (Act I, pp. 460–61). Is this some dreadful dream of death or some fragment of recollection from the madhouse? Yet out of the ruins of this woman comes the clear beauty of the last love scene.

> IRENE (*passionately*): No, no—high up in the glorious light; on the very summit of life's promise!
>
> RUBEK: There we shall celebrate our marriage, Irene—my beloved!
>
> IRENE (*proudly*): The sun shall witness it, Arnold.
>
> RUBEK: All the powers of light shall witness it; and all the powers of darkness too. (*Seizes her hand*) Bride of my spirit—will you follow me?
>
> IRENE (*as though transfigured*): I will follow my lord and master, with joy in my heart.
>
> RUBEK (*draws her after him*): We must first go through the mist, Irene—
>
> IRENE: Through the mist—yes. And then we shall stand at the very top of the tower that glitters in the sunrise.
>
> [Act III, pp. 498–99]

Notes

1. See *Letters of Henrik Ibsen,* trans. and ed. J. N. Laurvik and Mary Morison, p. 455. Also, *Hundreårsutgave Henrik Ibsens Samlede Verker,* ed. Francis Bull, Halvdan Koht, Didrik Arup Seip (Oslo: Gyldendal Norsk Forlag, 1928–57), 18: 447 (dated March 5): "De har i grunden ret når De siger at den serie, som afsluttes med epilogen, ag entlig begyndte med 'Bygmester Solness.' Men mere indgående wil jeg ikke gerne udtale mig om dette. Overlader alle kommentarer og tolkninger til Dem."

2. James Joyce said of the last play, "In this play, Ibsen has given us nearly the very best of himself. . . . On the whole, *When We Dead Awaken* may rank with the greatest of the author's work—if, indeed, it be not the greatest" (*The Critical Writings,* ed. Ellsworth Mason and Richard Ellmann [New York: Viking Press, 1959], p. 67). Archer's opinion was substantially different. See n. 6 below and pp. 28 and 30 above.

3. Sometime after he finished *Rosmersholm,* Ibsen told his friend Georg Brandes, the Danish critic, that he would write no more "polemical plays." Only *Lady from the Sea* (1888) and *Hedda Gabler* (1890) stood between that play and *The Master Builder.* See the introduction to Michael Meyer's translation of *Lady from the Sea* (London: Rupert Hart-Davis, 1960), p. 8.

4. Joyce also notes the resemblance of these women to those of earlier plays. See Joyce, *Critical Writings,* pp. 99–100.

5. Page references in quotations from the plays are to the translations by Eva Le Gallienne, *Six Plays by Henrik Ibsen* (New York: Modern Library, 1957) and *The Wild Duck and Other Plays by Henrik Ibsen* (New York: Modern Library, 1961).

6. Archer said of the play, "Essentially it is history of a sickly conscience, worked out in terms of pure psychology." See *The Collected Works of Henrik Ibsen,* trans. Edmund Gosse and William Archer (New York: Charles Scribner's Sons, 1912), 10: xxxi.

7. In this context, Solness is referring to the burning of the house.

8. The story originates with Dr. Julius Elias in an article in *Neue deutsch Rundschau,* December, 1906, p. 1462. In a conversation with Elias in February, 1891, Ibsen remarked, "Do you know, my next play is already hovering before me—of course in vague outline. But of one thing I have got firm hold. An experience: a woman's figure." The story, along with conjectures about the model for Hilde Wangel, is retold in Archer's introduction to the play, *Collected Works,* 10: xxiv–xxviii.

9. On the Rat-Woman see Richard Schechner, "The Unexpected Visitor in Ibsen's Late Plays," in *Ibsen: A Collection of Critical Essays,* ed. Rolf Fjelde (Englewood Cliffs, N.J.: Prentice-Hall, 1965), pp. 158 ff.

10. As a very young man, Ibsen wrote a poem expressing the same idea and using the same imagery. See *John Gabriel Borkman,* trans. Michael

Meyer (London: Rupert Hart-Davis, 1960), pp. 7–8. Another early poem
seems to foreshadow *The Master Builder*. See *Collected Works,* 10: xxii–
xxiii.

11. *Ibsen: The Last Plays,* trans. William Archer (New York: Hill &
Wang, 1959), pp. 155–56.

12. *Ibid.,* p. 156.

SELECTED BIBLIOGRAPHY

Bradbrook, Muriel Clara. *Ibsen the Norwegian: A Revaluation.* Hamden, Conn.: Archon Books, 1966.

Fjelde, Rolf, ed. *Ibsen: A Collection of Critical Essays.* Englewood Cliffs, N.J.: Prentice-Hall, 1965.

Ibsen, Henrik. *Letters of Henrik Ibsen.* Translated and edited by John Nilsen Laurvik and Mary Morton. New York: Duffield & Co., 1908.

Ibsen, Henrik. *Letters and Speeches.* Edited by Evert Sprinchorn. New York: Hill & Wang, 1964.

Koht, Halvdan. *The Life of Ibsen.* 2 vols. New York: American-Scandinavian Foundation, W. W. Norton & Co., 1931.

Muir, Kenneth. *The Last Plays of Shakespeare, Racine, and Ibsen.* Detroit: Wayne State University Press, 1961.

Shaw, G. B. *The Quintessence of Ibsenism.* New York: Hill & Wang, 1964.

Shakespeare

INTRODUCTION

Perhaps the most baffling quality about the last three plays of Shakespeare—I am disregarding *Pericles* because of its fragmentary authorship—is the blend of the fantastic and realistic elements of which they are composed. But surely hardly less mysterious is the homogeneous impression that they produce on the mind, and yet the impossibility of coming to grips with it in such a way that one can express any true sense of their "meaning." In fact this "meaning" is only truly conveyed by reading all the plays aloud. There is such a total blending of mood and subject matter that the bare description of themes, inadequate as it appears at any time in the discussion of Shakespeare, has a special sort of unsatisfactoriness here. In *The Tempest* it is clear that Shakespeare has written a play so subjective that perhaps the elements in it are not capable of bearing the weight of a fully impersonal interpretation. Yet, as so many critics have seen, perhaps no play conveys so surely the meaning of the universe, expressed and rendered in bodies and voices on the stage. And although *The Tempest* is the supreme triumph of its kind, neither *The Winter's Tale* nor *Cymbeline* is far behind.

37

To tease the imagination further, it is possible to distinguish in these last plays the final configuration of stories and motifs from the great tragedies. There are certainly echoes of *Othello* and *Lear*. As they have now become the stuff of something other than tragedy—to define the form no further—the change surely means something. What, dare we ask, is the final version? What is the meaning of the *mood* if we cannot find the theme separate from it?

Shakespeare is saying enough that is the same in these three plays—in the recurrence of the same sort of plot and figures in it—to permit us almost to speak of a world of the last plays. And the discordance of certain of the surface features, and our sense of it, can also be expressed. Perhaps this is our best way to a deepened understanding of the whole, to catch the hint of design at least momentarily separated from the completed work.

One can start by saying that the modern reader, and that rare creature the modern spectator—surely it is no accidental tribute to their difficulty that today of these plays only *The Tempest* is performed at all frequently—is subjected by their presentation to a peculiar jolting of his sensibilities. It is probably not worthwhile relating this to a contemporary mixture of tragedy and comedy. True, we know from Fletcher's defense of tragicomedy in the preface to *The Faithful Shepherdess,* and Jonson's support for his views, that the Jacobean theater was interested in plays that were serious in effect but technically differentiated from tragedy because death did not figure among the important incidents of the plot.[1] And, more important, Shakespeare himself had already experimented in *Measure for Measure* and even in *Troilus and Cressida* with a kind of play in which what was recognizable as a tragic or comic plot and characters were given twists which rendered the final effect not identifiable as clearly either. To say that Shakespeare's last plays blend tragedy and comedy in a contemporary Jacobean way is not to get us any further in describing our understanding of them. It is perhaps not even true. The plays, even in their pattern, seem unlike anything by anyone else of the time, and only superficially similar to Shakespeare's own early work.[2]

But it is more interesting to notice that for the reader or the audience there is uncertainty from the beginning about the kind of entertainment to be provided him. Both *Cymbeline* and *Winter's Tale* start as though one should expect a tragedy. Imogen's dilemma is sad enough, and she herself is no stock figure of medieval romance, a fair lady languishing in the absence of her true knight. She is flesh-and-blood and indeed one of the most moving heroines in Shakespeare after Desdemona.

> I did not take my leave of him, but had
> Most pretty things to say: ere I could tell him,
> How I would think on him at certain hours,
> Such thoughts and such: or I could make him swear
> The shes of Italy should not betray
> Mine interest and his honour; or have charg'd him,
> At the sixth hour of morn, at noon, at midnight,
> T'encounter me with orisons, for then
> I am in heaven for him; or ere I could
> Give him that parting kiss, which I had set
> Betwixt two charming words, comes in my father,
> And like the tyrannous breathing of the north,
> Shakes all our buds from growing.[3]
>
> [I, iv, 25–37]

This is as great, in tone as natural and compelling as

> That I did love the Moor, to live with him,
> My downright violence and storm of fortunes
> May trumpet to the world.
>
> [I, iii, 245–47]

But the second part of the play, beautiful as it is, this Arcadia inhabited by the unknown princes, the scene of their dialogues with their father on the merits of rusticity as opposed to the court—our Imogen's entry into it and her supposed death there are all quite different from the tone of her speech quoted above. They call for a different sort of response from the reader and the spectator, and, especially for the latter, the adjustment must be too rapid to be easy. The last part of *Cymbeline* all too clearly shows that Shakespeare is bored with the conclusion of the plot; its threads are wound up in the quickest and most perfunctory manner, the confusions are explained in a way that is at once repetitious and dull. Evidently whatever is important about the play does not lie in the story, in the ultimate fate of the characters, even of that Imogen for whom we care so much at the beginning. For in the second and third parts of the plot our feelings are not stirred by a threat to the existence of the characters we loved. Reality is restricted to the first part of the play. What we experience afterwards is a response in some sense different from sympathetic emotion.

The same is true of *The Winter's Tale*. Nowhere in Shakespeare, not in the greatest moments of *Lear* and *Othello,* is the horror radiating outward from the distortion of man's mental processes so solidly represented as in Leontes' self-torturing fantasies. Nowhere can one also see to such a frightening degree what they can do to people other than their unhappy possessor. The lines that convey Leontes' agony are really ugly.

> And many a man there is (even at this present,
> Now while I speak this) holds his wife by th' arm,
> That little thinks she has been sluic'd in's absence
> And his pond fish'd by his next neighbour, by
> Sir Smile, his neighbour....
>
> [I, ii, 192–96]

Yet the second part of the story, with its country festival and the panoply of shepherds and shepherdesses, however clothed in the genuine colors of the English countryside, has taken us into a world of make-believe very far from the terrors of Leontes.

The third part, with its wild fantasy of the living statue of Hermione, is even further removed from the emotion that waits upon Leontes' rages and the lot of his victims.

There is, then, in the plays a framework which changes and shifts, altering our expectations from one moment to the next. But apart from this, certain of the jolts are administered by a particular event or character which tears apart the mood into which we have fallen. Cloten is never a comfortable figure. It is difficult to know whether he should be played as a very boorish and stupid court type or someone mentally even duller than this. But his intention of ravishing Imogen in the clothes of her lover is something that carries one straight out of any capacity for laughing at him in the earlier scenes where Imogen banters him. Most disconcerting of all is the grotesqueness of the scene in which Imogen takes his headless body for that of Posthumus, assuring us that she would know it anywhere! To crown the effect, the boys sing the entrancingly beautiful "Fear no more the heat o' th' sun" over the seeming corpse of Imogen. In these instances and in others including the scenes involving Iachimo and his ambush in the chest, Shakespeare has deliberately chosen to combine incidents and images which must at first appear ill-suited, and which cumulatively constitute the representation of the world from a peculiar and novel angle, if it has any coherence at all.[4]

Can one clarify the image as theatrically projected any further? Perhaps. There would seem to be a divorce, in levels of treatment, between the plot, which expresses the arrangement of the characters in their interaction, and in their fates, and the characters themselves. The characters are "real"—that is, in most cases, they express in their persons a complicated truth which can only be conveyed by an actor physically and vocally in front of us who acts as a human being like ourselves. He cannot be solely a *suggestion* of a human being for the exposition of an intellectual or impersonal truth. But the story of what happens to him is no

longer designed to make us participate directly in his fortunes
with the eagerness and sympathy which they should excite in us
as people. The complexity of the action and the interdependence
of its parts are not there at all or else negligently executed and
in its place comes a pattern which must, I think, be symbolic.[5]

In both of the first two plays, *Cymbeline* and *Winter's Tale,*
the design is the same. The first part is the wicked old world
where the original evil act is launched; the second shows a "naturally" good world existing somewhere else and sheltering persons
who will eventually reform or replace the wrongdoers of the
first; the third deals with the redress of the original evil, and
the "purification" of the old world in the light of the "natural"
good of that rural Arcadian image of the second stage. In *The
Tempest* two of the parts, the first and the third, are represented
only vestigially. The wrong done to Prospero in banishing him
from his dukedom we only learn from himself—though perhaps
we catch a glimpse of the brutal state of nature involved in such
wrongdoing in the scene on shipboard and the disobedience of the
crew. The last part, the righting of the wrongs and the reinstatement of Prospero, comes to us only in his last speech on
his retirement to Milan. The play itself is an extended study of
part two, but with the elements of the "real" or perhaps we
should call it more "ordinary" world reintroduced at a strange
new level.[6]

We can spell out a common pattern in the plot of these plays.
We can at least notice some of the divergent elements in their
effects on us. Is it possible to say anything important about a
common theme or themes which run through them—anything
which would make us understand better what Shakespeare
"meant" by the last three plays?

Perhaps the broadest statement of the theme which emerges
might be: the power of man to make what he will of the world,
by means of political authority, or the force of his mind, or by
virtue of some sort of fantasy which can be called magic. This

theme spans the ill-judging despotism of Cymbeline (who represents the worst of conventional power), the tyranny and pathological fantasies of Leontes, the jealousy wager of Posthumus and Iachimo, the blend of political, imaginative, and magical power in Prospero, and the natural wickedness and natural affinity with beauty in the mind of the "natural" subject Caliban.

Political power figures largely—the capacity of a single man to impose his ordinary or extraordinary wishes on others, independent of the validity of his judgment, or the relation of this judgment to the real circumstances. But so, too, does the power of the imagination, in the form of either the personal hallucination or the ritualized versions of art or magic. The antagonist of this freedom of man to do what he will with his fellows or his world is reality, and reality exists as the truth of actual events, as time and as death.

All the plays explore the tension between these elements of reality and the utmost extent of the ruler's power in this world or man's ability to project himself mentally into another where they are inoperative.

The plot concerns a wrong done in the political world. Sometimes as in the first two plays it is a wrong done by the king to others, in the last it is a wrong done to Duke Prospero. There is a suggestion that the wrong is not singular. It is typical of a court life defaced by greed, foulness, flattery, every kind of untruth and ugliness. This is to be eventually succeeded by the vision of a new world, in which the old king will be replaced or reformed, and where the power will then belong to a young couple, and to the innocence of youthful bravery and virginity. This couple grows up in a setting and an atmosphere simple and primitive and very different from the crookedness and artificiality of the existing court. But the young couple is not to deal with a world completely different from that of their predecessors. It is reformed in certain respects; it is better; but there is more than a doubt in the representation of it, and the new rulers, that the same difficulties and the same wrongs may recur. What is objectively hopeful and better is that they are young, new, untried.

But the original wrong itself—can it be righted? What is the meaning of the righting of an old wrong—the injury done to Imogen and Posthumus by Cymbeline or that done by Posthumus himself to Imogen? Most telling: what is the righting of the wrong done by Leontes to his daughter Perdita and his wife Hermione? When Perdita finds her lover and they stand as successors to the kingdom, perhaps the original wrong has found a compensation in the scale of the universe. But what of Hermione herself, and the frustrated hopelessness of the criminal Leontes seeking expiation? If death is the end of life, and death is not only the final moment but the process which is time, it is not the same man who did the wrong who pays, nor the same person who is paid. Hence the ironical symbol of the living statue of Hermione, the hopeless incitement to a belief that one can start the same story over again in another way.

Lastly, what of the power of man's mind to transfer him, free, beyond the limits of "reality" and death? These plays express this in both good and bad directions—in the perverse self-torture of Leontes and the magical dramatizations of Prospero. The magic of Prospero, both in achieving his ends and giving entertainment, leads to the subject of drama itself, and the famous comparison of the perishability of the "real" world and the world of the stage and its creations. Yet it is the "real" world that wins. The time on the island is limited, the period of the magic is limited; Prospero, again Duke, returns to Milan where every third thought will be of his death.

If one asks oneself finally for a judgment on the mood of these plays—and a single mood they have—we must I think agree more nearly with the earlier critics than with Strachey.[7] The conclusion of the power theme is the replacement of the battle-scarred and disappointed and broken by the young who are intact and hopeful. But this description of the atmosphere of the plays is too broad and too crude. Half of what these plays "say" is not said through the mechanical turns of the plot, the destiny of the characters for good or ill, but through the peculiar air of the whole. And here optimism is the wrong word for what we find. There is a final happiness in the nature of life itself, there are haunting images of different sorts of eternity and immortality— but there is no great joy in man's individuality as such, nor its capacity to breed good in the world. The vision is one of muted happiness, but this belongs to the potential of man's mind and the eternal objective hope of each new beginning rather than to actual achievement. The author of *Lear* and *Macbeth, Coriolanus* and *Timon,* had not entirely outlived the meaning of these tragedies. The likelihood of man's error is all on the tragic side. The evil in his nature, the inherent evil and confusion in the physical world and social life, the ambiguity of man's two greatest assets, his sexuality and his imagination, and their ominous conjunction under the direction of a defective will and a mistaken judgment, all of this shows through the happiness of the issue in the plots of the last plays. In their ambience they live somewhere between the early comedies like *Midsummer Night's Dream* and *As You Like It* and the black plays like *Measure for Measure* and *All's Well That Ends Well.* The truth of the world must be expressed by covering more than man and his fate on earth. There must be taken into account the dreams and myths of half-forgotten pasts, and almost unimaginable futures—for the meaning of the human condition, if it is to be a joyful meaning, as Shakespeare finally thought it, must lean more on what might be, and the power of imagination to conceive that, than on what is. The cosmic reality of the joy must live in the image alongside that of the individual and subjective evil of the human creature. The reality of cruelty and tears must be represented as blended with laughter. Man's understanding of beauty must be tempered by his shock at seeing it in conjunction with ugliness. "Thersites' body is as good as

Ajax',", when neither is alive and the Caliban of "The isle is full of noises" is the brutish creature who tried to violate Miranda and would have peopled the island with Calibans. Caliban himself is both helpless victim and barely restrained savage animal. The tortured passion of Leontes is the other side of the faculty of Prospero, and the world itself may have no more solidity than the "cloud capp'd towers the gorgeous palaces" of the theater.

The note of optimism, then, is always tempered, uncertain, almost melancholy, never assertive. Shakespeare's joy is a hesitant hope: it must, to survive, live in the philosophic hesitation between hint and certainty. And it must find its expression, not in the imitation of the processes of the real world, all too surely indications of what is worst, but in the note of lyricism and fantasy, the poetic creation of another order of being. In man's capacity to conceive this lies the hope of its joyful meaning.

Cymbeline

Cymbeline is a play concerned with the righting of wrongs. The title suggests that the wrong is that done by Cymbeline to his daughter and her lover. The first scene seems to confirm this. But there is indeed a pattern of wrongs and insults, their consequences and reparations, all over the play. There is the cruel wrong done to Imogen by Posthumus. There is Belarius stealing his sons from Cymbeline in retaliation for Cymbeline's even more shadowy injuries to Belarius. The wrongs done to Imogen and Posthumus by Iachimo, and those to the Romans by the British, are there too. All these acts are to be righted or paid for by the end of the play. What is meant by the righting of wrongs, what is involved when an injury is made good or forgiven, this is a theme continuously present. It is the formal theme of the play—that expressed obviously by the action of the plot.

But also it is clear that the play as a whole shows consistently some sort of opposition between the natural and the conventional or artificial. Classifications and titles—what is covered by them and what is not—are very important. King and subject, imperial nation and subject nation, prince and commoner, these distinctions count for everything in the life of the court which constitutes much of the play. And there are the conventions governing love, the standard conceptions of purity in woman and knightliness in man; the rules of friendliness and the rules of war. On the other side, that of nature, the play treats with emphasis the relations of fathers and children, brothers and sisters. Finally it illustrates what may perhaps be called the life of natural man in the society

47

of his fellows instead of the elaborate hierarchy of the civilized world.

The plot, as such, does not carry us breathless, waiting on the event for those we love or hate, as it did in the great tragedies. Instead it saturates the mind with the repetition of the same pattern, and finally we come to know the people and look through the actions to the misty outline of a meaning for both. Single scenes become more important than the succession of them. In fact the unit of appreciation seems to be the scene. Iachimo's emergence from the chest, Imogen's approach to the cave of Belarius—such scenes as these stand out in all their expressiveness from the actions which precede them or follow from them. And within the scenes themselves there is no real movement; they do not *flow*. They arrest the mind in some perceptible compass of reference. Yet the restriction of meaning is not the ordinary one, which ties the meaning of the scene to the dramatic context of the various characters. Here the words and deeds of the characters blend with one another and with the atmosphere to form a new meaning for the world. The sense of Iachimo's scene, where he comes out of the chest into Imogen's bedroom, is of the luxuriant burgeoning of evil, of sensual enjoyment unfettered by moral responsibility. The beauty of his words, the uncanny wonder of the moment when he springs from the chest, merge. His words are not in themselves the effective expression of a villain. Indeed Iachimo himself is too flimsy a creation to be an effective villain in our world of illusion. But the words and dramatic moment do convey powerfully the horror of rank, poisonous emotion, no less frightening because it is impersonal and a bit fairy-like instead of the more solid and human wickedness of, say, Iago.

Furthermore, the significant colors which go to make up the livery of a concept are blended together of different sources. We are not allowed to keep those of the individual characters apart in order to cherish them as people not responsible for what we dislike in the total picture. Iachimo's sadistic poetry of the chest

scene is supplemented by Posthumus' speech against women as he
imagines the encounter of Iachimo and Imogen:

> Me of my lawful pleasure she restrain'd,
> And pray'd me oft forbearance: did it with
> A pudency so rosy, the sweet view on't
> Might well have warm'd old Saturn; that I thought her
> As chaste as unsunn'd snow. O, all the devils!
> This yellow Iachimo, in an hour, was't not?
> Or less; at first? Perchance he spoke not, but
> Like a full-acorn'd boar, a German one,
> Cried "O!" and mounted; found no opposition
> But what he look'd for should oppose and she
> Should from encounter guard.
>
> [II, iv, 161–71]

In his attitude toward women Posthumus is a very different
man from Iachimo, but they are both only elements in the same
impression of sexual passion with which the poet is imbuing us.
We gain nothing by harking back to the dramatic personality of
the two men and telling ourselves that Posthumus is the deceived
and Iachimo the deceiver. We are being given a view of woman's
sexual life seen through masculine eyes. It has two main characteristic expressions—a gross naturalness (the feminine receptiveness of the German boar) and the sophisticated cruelty of what
follows, the imagined gift of the bracelet to the new lover. This,
the "meaning" of love, by the force of the poetry and the dramatic
weighting of the scene far overrides the particular circumstances
of Iachimo or his character or that of Posthumus and even the fact
of Imogen's innocence.

Yet the characters, although much less developed and less articulated than in the great tragedies, count for something as characters. It seems as though certain tones and moods belong to each
character, and these are contrasted and blended with others or
matched against one another. There is an inclination too to represent character itself as a certain immobile moment of intensity in

emotion. The figures do not gradually define themselves in a sequence of actions leading to a peak: the intervening steps between their introduction and the peak are glossed over; it is the peak and this only that defines Cloten, Posthumus, Iachimo, even Imogen for us. And there is usually nothing that follows.[8] The future destiny of the characters, after we have appreciated the special contribution they have made to our understanding of the play by their passionate moment, is unimportant.

Cymbeline is a kind of power person. He represents, as Leontes and Polixenes are to do in *Winter's Tale,* a tyrant who is stupid, inefficient, often jealous and unfair. But he is the conventional holder of power, and such power, the power of the monarch, is the necessary element in civilized society. This power remains unquestioned and imperturbable. He is the legitimate king. It is, indeed, rather interesting that in all three of the last plays power is not represented in its origins and dynamic development as far as the monarch is concerned. In this the difference between them and the chronicle plays is very marked. Here the poet deals only with the monarch's personality insofar as he actually wields absolute and unalterable authority. (This extends also to Prospero, in whom the source of the power is magic.) Hence power is not considered as it is subject to change but as a permanent factor. You do not reflect on how this king or that gets power, but only on what he is like when he has it.

Cymbeline is an unpleasant king, as everything at his court is unpleasant. He decides to murder the prisoners of war, and we barely believe, in the beaming cheerfulness of the end, that he was deterred. When he makes ready to kill Cloten's murderer, he is turned from his purpose only by the assurance that the rank of the murderer was superior to that of the murdered. His stupid attitude toward the imperial power of Rome—for Shakespeare like Fletcher in *Bonduca* wants us to see it as stupid and uncivilized, in spite of the patriotic speeches of Cloten—is mitigated only by the authority of the oracle. His own explanation at the end is that all his wrongdoing is the result of deception by his wicked queen. The queen will do as an excuse as well as anything else. Shakespeare troubles very little to make that lady credible. He merely wants her as a prop, in this case a very bad one, for the conventional brutal and incompetent monarch. This is a king who understands nothing, who always mistakes the superficial for the deeper motive, whose only rule of action other than following his personal passions is obedience to the most standardized formulation of a court code.

Everything personal is underplayed in Cymbeline's relations to everyone. It might have been possible to make something of his feelings for his daughter whom he victimized. The First Gentleman in the first scene indeed tells us that Posthumus' success and Cloten's failure to win Imogen has caused no genuine sorrow except for the king "though I think the king be touch'd at very heart." But this leads nowhere. His anger against Posthumus and Imogen is Lear over again minus all the equivocal and ambiguous coloring which gives Lear personality in that opening scene. By contrast Cymbeline is simply the outraged prince whose authority has been flouted by his daughter and a subject. Shakespeare cares so little about developing the side of Cymbeline's attitude to Imogen that he never shows him doing anything effective about her disappearance. After learning that she is not to be found, he exclaims, "Grant, heavens, that which I fear prove false." But though he threatens Pisanio he carries the matter no further, and when at Act IV, scene iii, he exclaims about his bewilderment and bedevilment with queen sick, daughter gone, stepson gone, and the war on his hands, it is really a list of difficulties. We are not aware that Imogen is any more than an undifferentiated item on it. No, Cymbeline is rendered perfunctorily except as he plays the role of king—as master of the court, as leader in diplomacy, as commander-in-chief. In all these functions he is important and in all of them he represents conventional reasoning at its face value and therefore at its stupidest.

On Cloten the two key passages seem to come from Imogen and Belarius. As Pisanio pleads with Imogen's despair he says, "If you'll back to the court . . . ," and she answers:

> No court, no father, nor no more ado
> With that harsh, noble, simple nothing,
> That Cloten, whose love-suit hath been to me
> As fearful as a siege.
>
> [III, iv, 132–35]

And Belarius has this to say,

> . . . Long is it since I saw him,
> But time hath nothing blurr'd those lines of favour
> Which then he wore: the snatches in his voice,
> And burst of speaking were as his. . . .
>   Being scarce made up,
> I mean, to man, he had not apprehension
> Of roaring terrors: for defect of judgment
> Is oft the cause of fear.
>
> [IV, ii, 103–12]

The impression that Cloten creates is of vacancy and the threat of something evil in the vacancy. The quality of this sort of man —if perhaps he is a sort of degenerate royal offshoot vaguely recalled by such related types as Bergetto in 'Tis Pity She's a Whore —is the mind of a twelve-year-old in the large physical frame of a strong man. What is uncomfortable about this Shakespearean creation is that what comes through as basic, as entirely natural, is what we would like to think of as perversity and degeneracy. Cloten equates his sexual pleasure with the misery of the girl—the joy obtained corresponds to the suffering of the victim. And the peculiar twist to the manner of it lies in Cloten's own childish passion for clothes. As a stage figure he lies somewhere between Iago and Caliban. He is much more superficially represented than the one, for his love-hatred toward Imogen is shown as clearly due to the slight to himself, whereas the sources of Iago's strange passion lie deeper and more obscure. But he is all too human in comparison with the monstrous Caliban, and consequently his plan for violating Imogen in the clothes of her husband is far more disgusting than Caliban's projected pleasure in peopling the isle with Calibans to pain Miranda's father.

Yet as a stage figure he sets any actor a hard task. Surely it would be hard to render convincingly the combination of fool, near moron, coward of the opening scenes with his soliloquy in Act III:

> I love, and hate her: for she's fair and royal,
> And that she hath all courtly parts more exquisite
> Than lady, ladies, woman; from everyone
> The best she hath, and she of all compounded
> Outsells them all.
>
> [III, v, 71–75]

The subtlety and explicitness of this passage would come as a great difficulty to an actor who had played the earlier conversations between Cloten and the courtiers with drive and enthusiasm. The tough patriotic speeches to the Roman delegation are also written with a force and eloquence which is clearly hard to reconcile with any consistent human presentation of the character.[9] But as the embodiment of contradictory but related passions, united by defect of intelligence and thereby reduced to a deplorably observable level, Cloten is comprehensible and convincing. His grave-bed with Imogen is one of the most horrible of symbolic happenings. He wishes to violate Imogen in Posthumus' garments, because of Imogen's expressed preference for the garments next her lover's skin over Cloten's whole physical being. In the end Imogen knows the reality of Posthumus' body so little that she takes Cloten's headless trunk, clothed according to plan in Posthumus' clothes, for that of her loved one. The "fear no more the heat of sun" is, truly, directed solely to the supposed corpse of Fidele, but Belarius puts both bodies in the same grave and Guiderius remarks, "Thersites' body is as good as Ajax',/ When neither are alive."

Iachimo represents a certain motiveless malignity that can surround masculine sexuality. Act I, scene iv, shows the attitude of men among men to their womenfolk—a possession which can be and must be endlessly tried and won or lost to the honor or discredit of the masculine possessor. The notion of the wager is straight out of a fairy story, but the conversation, and the feeling of the dialogue, is realistic and convincing in its realism. You do not here, in Iachimo, have the mysteriously indicated motives of Iago. This man is prepared to murder Leonatus where he is most vulnerable with no reason stronger than ordinary masculine competitiveness. All of Posthumus' fine attitudes—gallantry, generosity, and modesty—are predicated on ignorant assumptions, not personal knowledge, and the Iachimos of the world are constituted by nature to assail them successfully. This is strangely reinforced by the wonder of the scene in which Iachimo surveys the sleeping Imogen:

> The crickets sing, and man's o'er-labour'd sense
> Repairs itself by rest. Our Tarquin thus
> Did softly press the rushes, ere he waken'd
> The chastity he wounded. Cytherea,
> How bravely thou becom'st thy bed! fresh lily!
> And whiter than the sheets! That I might touch!
> But kiss, one kiss! Rubies unparagon'd
> How dearly they do 't: 'tis her breathing that
> Perfumes the chamber thus: the flame o' th' taper
> Bows toward her, and would under-peep her lids,
> To see th' enclosed lights, now canopied
> Under these windows, white and azure lac'd
> With blue of heaven's own tinct.

[II, ii, 11–23]

In the sensual poetry here the world is invoked as an accomplice of Iachimo. It is such a world as his like can work in. There is nothing personal in his villainy. He is only the spokesman of a feeling which is also expressed in the wager scene. The possession of the woman, the source of sensual delight, is entirely unassured by any personal ties, loyalty, or promise. What is natural is animal and indeed not strictly animal only but of the atmosphere and setting of the living creature. It is not without reason that Shakespeare loses interest in Iachimo after he has won his wager with Posthumus. His repentance, which is needed to adjust what is wrong and assert what is agreeable and right, is readily at the disposal of Posthumus, without even such equivocality as lies in Edmund's "Yet Edmund was beloved." From first to last there is nothing personal in Iachimo. It is therefore not necessary to make a character of him with reasons for his change of heart. He is of the moment when "the crickets sing, and man's o'er-labour'd sense repairs itself by rest." But he is also of that which is in some sense *real,* underlying the conventions regarding man's sexuality.[10]

Posthumus is a matching exhibition of conventional beliefs unsupported by any reality of personal conviction or knowledge. His is a mood of total trust rapidly turned at need to total jealousy and the willingness to murder. The closest parallel to Posthumus in the rest of Shakespeare is not Othello, with his complicated security and insecurity, but Troilus, the type of conventionally true lover who is betrayed by the generically false girl. The recollections of Cressida lie heavy on *Cymbeline:*

IACHIMO
She stripp'd it from her arm: I see her yet:
Her pretty action did outsell her gift,
And yet enrich'd it too: she gave it me,
And said she priz'd it once.

[II, iv, 101–4]

In Act II, scene iv, the bitterly obscene denunciation of women as the source of creation is the moment of self-torture which Shakespeare presents here with a fictitious base, as it is in Leontes',

and again, with reality to back it, in the scene where Troilus sees
Diomedes with Cressida. But in Posthumus, Shakespeare also allows one to see some thoughts on sexual morality, and punishment
for its infractions, which cast a curious light on the earlier scenes.
At Act V, scene i, Posthumus, overwhelmed with his guilt at
having, he believes, killed Imogen, reflects on the train of events
leading up to his command to Pisanio:

> Yea, bloody cloth, I'll keep thee: for I wish'd
> Thou should'st be colour'd thus. You married ones,
> If each of you should take this course, how many
> Must murder wives much better than themselves
> For wrying but a little? O Pisanio,
> Every good servant does not all commands:
> No bond, but to do just ones. Gods, if you
> Should have ta'en vengeance on my faults, I never
> Had liv'd to put on this; so had you saved
> The noble Imogen, to repent, and struck
> Me, wretch, more worth your vengeance. But alack,
> You snatch some hence for little faults; that's love
> To have them fall no more: you some permit
> To second ills with ills, each elder worse,
> And make them dread it, to the doers' thrift.
> But Imogen is your own.
>
> [V, i, 1–16]

There is nothing remotely like this in *Othello*. All of Othello's
misery springs from the realization that he has been fooled into
committing murder. There is no hint that, had the case been as
he originally conceived it, had Desdemona been Cassio's lover, he,
Othello, could in honor have acted differently from the way he
did. But this is not Posthumus' feeling at all. Suddenly the whole
incident, begun by the wager, appears to him a senseless and
trivial affair, for which he had exacted a life. He now thinks that
neither in the order of the world, as ruled by the gods, nor in
sensible human justice, can he find excuse. Sexual infidelity, in the
total sum of the acts of a life, or the color of a character, cannot

bear the weight which it is conventionally assumed to possess. There is a moment of reason and repentance when a man, any man (for indeed Posthumus is any man, and no particular person any more than Iachimo his destroyer is any particular person either) can gain a perspective which makes nonsense of the code of honor and vengeance affecting sexuality.

Shakespeare has no further use for Posthumus after this scene. He has to drag him through the battle in order to tie all the ends together. He must be honored by Cymbeline as he had formerly been discredited. His dream in the jail can be the occasion for a masque. But his part in the play is finished effectively at the beginning of Act V.[11]

Imogen's part is written with much greater purity and even harshness than the conventionalization of the fairy story would suggest.[12] The love poetry of "I would have broke mine eyestrings, crack'd them, but/ To look upon him" (I, iv, 16–17) is true love poetry and as powerful as any Shakespeare ever wrote. And she can hate as well as love with an unexpected depth of natural passion, considering the story. Here she is summing up her immediate reactions to Cloten: "I am sprited with a fool,/ Frighted and anger'd worse" (II, iii, 140–41). She loathes Cloten—just for being himself, rather than for anything he has done to her. Her dislike is so great that it leads her to the unlucky remark which stings the sadistic imaginings that lurk somewhere in Cloten's dim intelligence. She answers his disparagement of Posthumus:

> He never can meet more mischance than come
> To be but nam'd of thee. His mean'st garment,
> That ever hath but clipp'd his body, is dearer
> In my respect, than all the hairs above thee,
> Were they all made such men.
>
> [II, iii, 133–37]

Her part in the trial to which Posthumus' wager exposes her is that of deep feminine loyalty. Yet it is interesting to notice that neither lover emerges unscathed from Iachimo's stratagem. It is

not necessary to illustrate this for Posthumus, who succumbs at
once to his opponent's proofs. But although Imogen comes triumphant through her verbal encounter with Iachimo (partly,
surely, because of the extreme grossness of the line of attack)
something of the poison of Iachimo's slanders has penetrated her
mind and will not be banished. In Act III when Pisanio shows her
the letter from his master, her comment runs in part:

> Thou [Iachimo] didst accuse him of incontinency;
> Thou then look'dst like a villain: now, methinks,
> Thy favour's good enough. Some jay of Italy
> (Whose mother was her painting) hath betray'd him:
> Poor I am stale, a garment out of fashion,
> And, for I am richer than to hang by th' walls,
> I must be ripp'd:—to pieces with me!
>
> [III, iv, 47–52]

The rest of Imogen's part is not concerned with her relationship
with Posthumus. Shakespeare allows this to fall away from our
interest. There is really no sensible ground for Pisanio's suggestion
of a masculine disguise for her. She is merely going to wait
around until Posthumus' attitude toward her changes. For some
time, as far as the play goes, she is going to recede into an image
in the mind of Posthumus. When she emerges in the last reunion
and reconciliation she does so invested with all the attributes she
has acquired in her sojourn in the wilderness. And for this sojourn
the masculine disguise is necessary. This in fact is the reason for
it. She is going to find her brothers. The boys are to be a certain
kind of substitute for Posthumus.

> . . . would it had been so, that they
> Had been my father's sons, then had my prize
> Been less, and so more equal ballasting
> To thee, Posthumus.
>
> [III, vii, 48–51]

The "natural" recognition of brother and sister is emphasized, and
it is clear that the value of the family relationship is being

weighed in a scale against the free choice of sexuality. The Imogen that meets the finally repentant Posthumus has, dramatically, nothing to say to him in a personal way. When she rejoins her husband she has become almost a symbol compounded of what she originally was and the family ties she has discovered.

The only other characters of consequence are Pisanio and the queen. Pisanio is the figure of the good contriver and go-between, a sort of benevolent Machiavel, related to Camillo and Paulina in *Winter's Tale*. The queen is the evil genius on the other side. These are all puppets, though Pisanio and the queen more so than the *Winter's Tale* pair. As Shakespeare grew impatient with the realistic structure as an image of truth, he has recourse to dramaturgical tricks to cut and select what he wants to happen. Pisanio and the queen serve this purpose and are no more characterized than the bare necessity of their function demands.

The plot itself, even superficially, reveals glaring inadequacies. Could anything be more absurd than Pisanio's willingness to give his beloved mistress the box containing the drug confided to him by the deeply distrusted queen? Were ever the threads of a story pulled together with such haste and carelessness at the end? Even the given situation is absurd, in realistic terms, and Shakespeare actually has the audacity to laugh at it! Here is how the subject of the disappearance of Cymbeline's children is treated.

SECOND GENTLEMAN
That a king's children should be so convey'd,
So slackly guarded, and the search so slow
That could not trace them!

FIRST GENTLEMAN
Howsoe'er 'tis strange,
Or that the negligence may well be laugh'd at,
Yet is it true, sir.

[I, ii, 63–67]

A somewhat similar instance is the famous "Exit Antigonus pursued by a bear" in *Winter's Tale*. In both plays a certain event must be assumed to have taken place. Cymbeline's children must have been kidnapped; Antigonus must be got rid of. But Shakespeare will not trouble himself much about the why or the how of it. This is perhaps one of his reasons for being attracted to fairy stories in this last period. He wants a wider scope from which to draw the relevant strands of color and action than can be given him by realistic narrative.

For indeed the development of the plot itself is set against the importance of cause and effect, as they would be understood in the ordinary world—even, in a way, against the importance of sequence. Events happen and are significant; the hinges, on which the blocks of action turn, are not. We must know what Imogen feels both about her husband and about Cloten. We must understand the atmosphere of the wager scene in Rome. We must feel every implication of the moment when Iachimo comes out of the chest in Imogen's bedroom. We must be moved and horrified by the depth of Posthumus' passionate hatred when he thinks himself betrayed by Imogen, and by hers when she finds that he is willing to kill her. We must take in the meaning of his repentance and change of heart. Above all we must be entirely possessed by the spectacle of Imogen and Cloten sharing the same grave. But Shakespeare no longer thought that it mattered to write a plausible story that connected these events, not certainly in the way in which the stories of *Hamlet* or even *Lear* or *Othello* are connected. The audience or reader does not have to enter into the reality of the process of the story. His mind must be affected only by the conjunction of certain ideas, passions, sensations, characters— insofar as they are part of the scene. Of course, it is impossible to contrive even these short units of action without involving us in some continuity of a process with its causes and effects. The scene of the wager follows its course, reflecting the different emotions of the participants, to its conclusion in Iachimo's forcing Posthumus to the trial of Imogen. But the effect of each of the scenes is the diffusion of a certain atmosphere, or the expression of an idea through the contrast and interaction of a number of different people. The characters and their speeches merge in a common color or by their contrast attract our attention to some horrible disproportion. The wager scene leaves the impression of a false smoothness with danger lurking in it; of spite and heartlessness—there is no one who is not prepared to dislike Posthumus even before he appears—of a habitual temperature of coldness and dislike punctuated by the hope of a sensational crisis between possible rivals and competitors. It is a very uniform society and Posthumus is too innocent and too vulnerable to its attacks to escape. This is the outer face of the spiritual world whose inner reality is expressed by Iachimo's soliloquy in Imogen's bedchamber. Again, there are jarring elements clearly intended to call attention to themselves and thereby refer to a hidden reality which the fairy story reveals. The sequence involving the personality of Cloten (the first two scenes), the destiny of Cloten in his death by the mountainside, and Imogen's mistake about the body is one such. Certainly according to any surface realism this is, to say the least, improbable. But there is a sort of truth here which strikes through the layer of surface improbability to another depth. We feel the horror of Imogen's confusion of the headless body with that of Posthumus, as we felt the perversity of the beauty of "fear no more the heat of sun" when sung for Imogen and followed by "Thersites' body is as good as Ajax'" when both are dead. And we feel the horror and the perversity because Cloten has made upon us such an impression of clumsiness, ugliness, and sadism.[13]

As far as its construction goes, clearly this plot has three sections which have been welded together, from different sources.[14] One deals with Posthumus and the wager; one with Cymbeline and the British-Roman conflict; one with the "natural" Arcadian life of Belarius and his foster sons. Links have been forged to bind the three. Belarius has stolen the king's sons, whom he is bringing up in a setting far from the falseness and corruption of the court. Therefore, at some stage they must be restored and this means another encounter between Cymbeline and Belarius. Further, the battle is arranged to happen near the cave of the boys and their foster father and so their bravery can be made the decisive factor in the settlement of the war between Romans and Britons. Imogen is going to "find" her brothers and this unites her part of the story with that of Belarius. Iachimo, Posthumus' destroyer, is one of the generals leading the Roman side to Britain, and so Posthumus and his personal enemy can be brought together. The prophecy makes the end dependent on the solution of each of the several parts of the plot—the successful conclusion to the love trials of Posthumus and Imogen (the "lion's whelp" and the "piece of tender air"), the recovery of the children of Cymbeline ("the stately cedar" with "the lopped branches") and by implication the proper solution of the quarrel between Britain and Rome, "Britain shall be fortunate and flourish in peace and plenty." The mechanical links are only mechanical and indeed something worse: Shakespeare is not very particular about them and almost careless. In the end he is plainly trying to finish off the structural side of the plot with a scanty respect for its intricacies. Having to explain all its meanderings to Cymbeline is too much for him and with what looks uncommonly like the same spirit of caricature that marks the comment of the First Gentleman discussing the stealing of the king's children Cymbeline says:

> When shall I hear all through? This fierce abridgement
> Hath to it circumstantial branches, which
> Distinction should be rich in. Where? how liv'd you?
> And when came you to serve our Roman captive?
> How parted with your brothers? how first met them?
> Why fled you from the court? and whither?

> [V, v, 383–88]

It is hardly oversubtlety to see Shakespeare playfully calling our attention to the histrionic absurdity of the old kind of plot for his present purpose. The conditions of his stage make some version of the conventional story technique incumbent on him. He might not leave anyone's destiny unexplained, and everyone who comes to know anything must be shown to us as having learned it from some discernible source. But the author is both perfunctory and mischievous in his treatment.[15]

If the construction is flimsy and in places careless, the final impression of the cohesion of the bits and pieces is not.[16] First, there is the fact that nothing goes wrong in the end. Of course, with the atmosphere of the play set for us, we are prepared to see Imogen and Posthumus live happily ever after. But in addition, Cymbeline's sons are restored to him, and the quarrel between Rome and Britain fortunately allayed. There are no casualties except the wicked stepmother and Cloten. We will regret neither of them. The world is certainly better without this queen, and she is fortunately removed by sickness, without anyone's having to help nature's process. She even stages a deathbed confession that clears up any remaining difficulties to a happy conclusion. Iachimo also repents, in lines with such a curious series of emphases that it seems rather likely Shakespeare himself is slightly amused and means us to be so:

> Upon a time, unhappy was the clock
> That struck the hour: it was in Rome, accurst
> The mansion where: 'twas at a feast, O, would
> Our viands had been poison'd (or at least
> Those which I heaved to head) the good Posthumus
> (What should I say? he was too good to be
> Where ill men were, and was the best of all
> Amongst the rar'st of good ones) sitting sadly,
> Hearing us praise our loves of Italy....
>
> [V, v, 153–61]

Imogen takes the fatal drug and sleeps, but wakes again none the worse for her experiences, and Lucius and the other prisoners of war are sentenced to death but are happily reprieved.

All of this belongs with the fairy story and its "live happily ever after." But it must also in some important way express the author's vision, and this seems to mean that the *proper* conclusion of events, which are clearly headed for disaster and evil, is not disaster and evil but good. In this, *Cymbeline* and *The Winter's Tale* belong with *The Tempest*. Moreover, the happy endings in these three plays are different from those of the earlier doubtful comedies like *Measure for Measure,* where the happiness is barbed with ambiguity and sarcasm. It is nearly impossible to see the end of *Measure for Measure* without reflecting on the character of Isabella, on her relations with her brother and the Duke, on her sense of honor and her early strictness as a postulant. It is also nearly impossible not to wonder about the Duke's integrity throughout. Shakespeare has ironically pointed his finger at these aspects of his plot. But in *Cymbeline* there is no such sarcasm visible. At worst, there is playfulness in the rendering of Iachimo's repentance and Cymbeline's massive retractions. If there is a fault in *Cymbeline,* indeed, it is that too much of the ordinary world is still retained while the probability of the events is suspended. The conversation of Iachimo and his friends in Rome does not prepare us for Iachimo's later graceful repentance. Cloten and his toadies and his moronic obsessions come too near the real thing to blend with the wicked stepmother and the masque-dream of Posthumus. Some of these difficulties recur in *Winter's Tale*. It is only in *The Tempest* that Shakespeare has achieved the perfect blend of atmosphere with his new peculiar logic of events which conveys them to a good end. One knows that Prospero's magic will work successfully against Caliban. Ariel is in place in the enchanted island. But even in *The Tempest* the realistically ugly cannot and ought not to be banished. And Caliban, in his pathos, brutality, and perversity is the clue to the inclusion of Cloten and his headless trunk in *Cymbeline* and the terrifying obscenity of Leontes' passion in *Winter's Tale*. The ugly as an element in the world demands expression even in the optimistic vision of the fairy story.

Aside from the abortiveness of evil, the second emphasis in the play is decisively on the peculiar relations of nature and artifice—in man's values, pursuits, organizations, in society and in nations.

At first the overriding impression is that nature is good, and artifice is what introduces the elements of what is bad. Belarius joyfully proclaims the cleanness and freedom from treachery and malice of his life, and that of his foster sons, in the mountains. The simple existence of the hunter and the simple cave for a dwelling are agreeably free of the defects of which we have been very aware in the previous part of the play spent at Cymbeline's court. It certainly seems obvious that Imogen is right when she tells us that all her troubles would be over if she were a neatherd's daughter instead of a princess. The court is rotten with artifice—the courtiers disguising their sentiments toward Posthumus because of their respect for the king; Cloten's sycophantic attendants; Cloten himself with his concern about "derogating." In courts and cities, individual man is stifled by a network of rules, manners, conventions which choke what is good in him and invariably serve what is either trifling and frivolous or arrogant and cruel. The play also asserts the goodness of nature in ways beyond the mere opposition to artifice. Imogen finds a "natural" response to her brothers in her own heart and they to her. Their affection is described as a real makeweight to her loss of her lover, Posthumus. As they discover mutual affection, the "natural" evil of the stepmother toward her stepchildren also comes to light. Posthumus' repentance for the murder he tried to commit comes from a searching of his natural sentiments rather than a reliance on what society expects of him or allows him to do.

Yet as we understand the play better, the artificial forms of society cease to be, in a simple sense, the villains of the piece. At their best they are the external signs appropriate to a natural quality. The sons of Belarius are naturally impelled to the civilized life of the prince and the soldier and away from the primitive existence they have led. In their repudiation of their foster

father's arguments they give their best reasons for the concern
with form and artifice in human life.

ARVIRAGUS
                    What should we speak of
When we are old as you? When we shall hear
The rain and wind beat dark December? How
In this our pinching cave shall we discourse
The freezing hours away? We have seen nothing:
We are beastly: subtle as the fox for prey,
Like warlike as the wolf for what we eat:
Our valour is to chase what flies: our cage
We make a quire, as doth the prison'd bird,
And sing our bondage freely.

                                        [III, iii, 35–44]

Furthermore, at their least important the artificial norms of
behavior are some restraint on the animal cruelty and greed of
the ordinary everyday sort of prince—which Cymbeline is. It says
little for him that the argument which decides him in sparing
the life of Cloten's murderer is that the rank of the killer is
superior to that of his victim. But at least this legalism is a fetter.
The legalities of international pacts, between Britain and Rome,
the rights of prisoners of war, are always in jeopardy. They are
always just on the edge of being violated by the natural forces
of greed and aggressiveness. But they are the only barriers that
stand, however uncertainly, between these forces and their un-
limited exercise. Form, at its best, is the expression of the ideal
in man's ordinary life, individual and social. At its least effective,
it is still a restraint. But form is also the degeneration of the
substance of that life—and this is of course far commoner than
the other aspect. For Cloten the distinction of the prince lies in
his clothes (on which, grimly, so much is made to turn in the
conclusion), in the official titles of those with whom he con-
verses, and on the ritual of conversation with them. He is that
"harsh, noble, simple nothing" Cloten.

Furthermore, nature is not, as we at first supposed, itself a guarantee of goodness. There are horrors as "natural" as the healthy simplicity of Belarius' life in the wilderness. The sadism of Cloten's wish to rape Imogen in the presence of her murdered husband is unfortunately as "natural" as the wolflike appetites denounced by Arviragus. And such natural evil borrows protection of the forms for its characteristic manifestation. Cloten's determination to conduct the rape while he wears Posthumus' clothes is part of his preoccupation with clothes and titles which has been used by Imogen for her barbed witticism at his expense. Iachimo's plan to cuckold Posthumus or at least to convince him that he has been cuckolded is as natural as the cunning of the fox in pursuit of his quarry. But the form of its execution in the wager scene, the tempting of Imogen (which is a kind of verbal debauchery at her expense), and the manufacture of the convincing evidence all belong where a debased imagination works through the forms of what man has conceived of as expressing himself and the truth of the world at their highest.

In such stories of fantasy, traditional or invented, the ugly tendency of events or the inevitability of ugly thoughts issuing in ugly deeds may be controlled and reversed. Shakespeare's latest vision of the truth implies that some order and beauty rule events which through them possess meaning. That meaning may be impenetrable to man's reasoning intellect. It can be presented and apprehended with its appropriate doubts and ambiguity, in the images of poetry, in the fairy atmosphere where good and virtue can be represented as artificially triumphant. As a skeleton for his new form of theatrical creation this was exactly right.

What is it then that holds this play together? Is there any way to describe critically what we feel to be the *meaning* of the play?

Perhaps it might be called a parable of man, self-impelled to artifice to express in his living what is best and worst in his nature; and how the end of every story of him, as person, ruler, or nation so conditioned by the struggle of nature and art, must be both good and miraculous. Good, because the evil in man is not matched by a strong enough evil in the nature of the universe of which he is part, because, though the balance in favor of the survival of beauty, the increase of understanding, the rule of law is very slight, yet the balance tilts that way and not the other. Miraculous, because nobody sensitive enough to the complexity of human beings can believe that ordinary human causes operating in this world guide matters to such a favorable end. The fairy story and the myth and the more individual exercise of human fantasy are the likeliest molds for the playwright's meaning, hesitating as they do between the necessary pessimism bred of a knowledge of man and any theological doctrine that would assure us of a comprehensibly good purpose for the universe.

The Winter's Tale

The first overriding impression of *The Winter's Tale* must surely be the extraordinary power of the poetry and the compression and neatness of the structure. However one may judge the play most truly—as tragedy, ironic comedy, or fantasy—one knows firmly and immediately that it is entirely successful in producing its effect. This is really most surprising in view of what looks like the impossibility of the task which the play sets the actor and director. Hermione pretends to be a statue, appears on the stage as such, and descends from her pedestal to greet the husband she has not known for sixteen years. Leontes' pathological jealousy is presented with elaborate clinical detail through three acts, during which the audience is thoroughly conditioned to the acceptance of this dramatic atmosphere. But the next act transfers us to the Arcadian scene of the sheepshearing in Bohemia and Perdita's famous speech on English flowers. The figure of Autolycus and his connection with the shepherds are marvellous as comedy but it is not immediately apparent how they are to be integrated in the general effect. There are Camillo and Paulina uneasily hovering between being stage mechanisms and fully developed human beings. These are a few of the problems which have clearly frightened away many directors and actors, for the play is presented very rarely.

And yet, strangely enough, it *is* intensely theatrical, and even a mediocre performance shows that. The resurrection of Hermione must correspond with some genuinely dramatic aspect of the truth, for the actress *can* descend and greet Leontes without being ridiculous. In fact, the action awakens a strange degree of complicated emotion. Leontes and the Bohemian scene are proper partners seen against some wider reality than either, and the gaiety, irony, and toughness of the role of Autolycus is exactly the mediating Chorus required by the shift. The ambiguity of Camillo and Paulina haunts the story, though in a slight and shadowy way, so that we seem to be seeing real life transformed into a fairy tale or a fairy tale coming alive.

Perhaps indeed this is what it is—a fairy story that exposes human roots and in so doing reflects on itself. The questions it suggests—or more truly the equivocalities it brings to life in its stage being—are: What can man's mind do in transforming the world for himself and those around him? What is the limit of a reality shared with others which establishes the difference between madness and imagination? What actions once done can man's imagination undo, effectively? What part of reality cannot be dislodged by any fantasy and must be expressed in humor and irony? What human passions belong so to the order of reality—greed, vindictiveness, hatred—that they remain stubbornly part of man when the fairy tale comes alive, and in coming alive expresses the truth inherent in its existence?

In this play it is the quality of the poetry which carries the dramatic life of the piece. The poetry of the Leontes part is given over to cruelty, torturing misery, and above all the sense of obsession.

> Nor night, nor day, no rest: it is but weakness
> To bear the matter thus: mere weakness. If
> The cause were not in being,—part o' th' cause,
> She, th' adultress: for the harlot king
> Is quite beyond mine arm, out of the blank
> And level of my brain, plot-proof: but she
> I can hook to me: say that she were gone,
> Given to the fire, a moiety of my rest
> Might come to me again.
>
> [II, iii, 1–9]

Here is the evil creative power of the mind, made visible and convincing. It is not only speech by a character revealing that he is evil and jealous. The words and the rhythms are themselves alive; they are the substance of weary self-devouring agony. What is needed against this—for the peculiar vision of this play—is the *poetic* assurance of the young life that has survived in its beauty and hope. And that is Perdita and the sheepshearers, and the evocation of the English countryside in its flowers. As George Orwell says, there is nothing more characteristic of the English than the love of flowers,[17] and it would seem to have been no less true for the England of the Jacobeans. This is the touch of reality, the natural sense of beauty that blends with the more formalized concept of Arcadia, that still holds the whole in some region that can be relevant to the dreadful words and deeds of Leontes. In the third part, the poetic fantasy which has previously taken shape as Leontes' diseased imagination and then as the stylized rural paradise shifts to the statue. What is the statue— a clumsy stage device to express Paulina's stratagem? Surely not only this. But it is not a representation of magic either. It lives in some ambiguous mood where one must ask oneself whether the live-dead woman is Leontes' distorted dream of repentance, touched by the ironic reality of the actually developing wrinkles, or some symbol necessary to the final scene of reunion of the old and the new, the mother and the daughter who is her replacement.

By way of contrast with *Cymbeline* the plot appears coherent and close-knit. Paradoxically, this may be because Shakespeare has moved further away from the older straightforward narrative form. These three parts—Sicilia, Bohemia, and Sicilia again—are really discrete and can be balanced against one another because the author boldly presents them to us as *his* work, as the pictures that *he* wants us to look at in succession to understand his meaning. Time, in the person of a chorus, intervenes to set the stage for the second part, and directs our attention to the lapse of sixteen years and the concerns of Perdita. We are formally disassociated from Leontes and the episodes which filled in the first movement of the play. Indeed, by a rather barefaced stratagem within the drama, we are invited to just such an excursion in the first act when Archidamus addresses his opposite number, Camillo, and observes: "If you shall chance, Camillo, to visit Bohemia, on the like occasion whereon my services are now on foot, you shall see, as I have said, great difference betwixt our Bohemia and your Sicilia" (I, i, 1–4). The reader, or audience will indeed make the trip, and will in certain respects find Bohemia and Sicilia very different, but assuredly not in the person of the rulers of each realm. For in Bohemia we are asked to see the injury done by his father to Florizel and his bride as a paler example of the same sort of tyranny that Leontes practiced on his wife and infant daughter. The two kings were, we are told, brought up together. They have been lifelong friends. Having left us in the first part sympathetic with Polixenes, the play goes on to show him in the same role of persecutor as that from which he has himself escaped. Of course, the example is paler. It is paler in the same fashion that Gloucester shadows Lear.

The tyrannical acts of the first king spring from an altogether personal and peculiar character, those of the second are the conventional cruelties of the angry father. The actions of each are examples of tyranny, the power of the monarch to do what he pleases—and in the unexpectedness of the harshness of both kings we are made to feel the same sensation of helplessness of the victims who find their plans and their lives suddenly turned topsy-turvy because of a change in mood on the part of another man. The third part explicitly unites the problems of the first two for solution, as Camillo obligingly explains to us. In its extraordinary way, and in its extraordinary mood, it brings together all the victims, confronts them with their persecutors, settles the value of the repentance and the nature of the absolution, and does all this while looking across a great gulf at the original actions of which we have been spectators. The subject of each part is clearly developed: there is really no running over from one to the other; there is no need, as in *Cymbeline,* for events that we as audience know perfectly well to be explained at length to some actor in the drama.

The first part—all of the play to the end of Act III—is intensely detailed in its human treatment and intensely realistic.[18] Leontes, Hermione, even Mamillius; Camillo and Polixenes (here); Paulina and her husband Antigonus; every one of them is alive. Yet their liveliness as people and actors exists under the shadow of a threat that broods only half-explained, humanly, over the complex scene. This jealousy of Leontes is not only in itself without explanation of origin. It becomes a horror almost separable from Leontes, its agent. It tortures him as it tortures everyone else including us that watch and read in the spirit of watching. It is half there in the shadows when his mother urges the child Mamillius to tell her a story and he chooses one of spooks and goblins, and starts, "There was once a man . . . who lived by a churchyard," to be interrupted by the entrance of his crazy father beset by phantoms far more convincing than the

goblins of romance. It is evoked, nourished, ebbs, and swells
in the poetry, until it finally falls crushed, leaving us and Leontes
sick and wearied, with the words of the Delphic oracle, the death
of the boy, the assumed death of Hermione and the last formal
impersonal drained speech of the king.

> Thou didst speak but well
> When most the truth: which I receive much better
> Than to be pitied of thee. Prithee, bring me
> To the dead bodies of my queen and son:
> One grave shall be for both: upon them shall
> The causes of their death appear, unto
> Our shame perpetual. Once a day I'll visit
> The chapel where they lie, and tears shed there
> Shall be my recreation. So long as nature
> Will bear up with this exercise, so long
> I daily vow to use it. Come, and lead me
> To these sorrows.
>
> [III, ii, 232–43]

But though the jealousy becomes almost a disembodied force
that controls the scene, and lives in the poetry with a power
which is not altogether rooted in the dramatic personality of
Leontes, that jealousy in Leontes the man is expressed with the
most complicated clinical detail. Leontes is someone bent on his
own ruin. The causelessness of the jealousy is exactly what is
most important. Leontes himself is aware of this and tries in
his crazy fashion to guard against suspicion. He says to Camillo:

> Dost think I am so muddy, so unsettled,
> To appoint myself in this vexation; sully
> The purity and whiteness of my sheets,
> (Which to preserve is sleep, which being spotted
> Is goads, thorns, nettles, tails of wasps)
> Give scandal to the blood o' th' prince, my son,
> (Who I do think is mine and love as mine)
> Without ripe moving to 't?
>
> [I, ii, 325–32]

Shakespeare has made four remarkable studies of sexual jealousy—Troilus, Othello, Posthumus, and Leontes. In the minds of all the victims the typical images of their plight, as the cuckold, are much the same. But Leontes stands out in that *his* mind generates them without any outside stimulation. Here there is no Iachimo or Iago, much less the sight of Cressida and Diomedes. Some terrible wish for his own destruction possesses him. What he seeks is the drama of a protracted agony and a fitting conclusion. And he is convincing at every moment of it. Nothing is clearer proof, dramatically, that this is what Shakespeare is expressing through Leontes than our immediate readiness to accept his words as truly descriptive of his condition. *We* never, like Camillo, want to know what makes him think the way he does. We can see at once that Camillo is being stupid, even if understandably so, in trying to discover some factual source in Leontes' suspicion. We have known and entered into his madness from the first moment we have heard the opening note of the tremendous speech:

> Too hot, too hot!
> To mingle friendship far, is mingling bloods.
> I have *tremor cordis* on me: my heart dances,
> But not for joy—not joy. This entertainment
> May a free face put on, derive a liberty
> From heartiness, from bounty, fertile bosom,
> And well becomes the agent: 't may, I grant:
> But to be paddling palms, and pinching fingers,
> As now they are, and making practis'd smiles,
> As in a looking-glass; and then to sigh, as 'twere
> The mort o' th' deer—O, that is entertainment
> My bosom likes not, nor my brows.

[I, ii, 108–19]

This fantasy of Leontes has to spread until it covers his whole life, as father, husband, king. Only so can he establish himself in the twofold role he wants—the greatly injured and the greatly vengeful. Hence the successive steps: the assumption of Hermione's guilt with Polixenes; then Camillo's association with Polixenes; then the plot of all of them to murder him; then the bastardy of Perdita. But the process takes place at some level significantly different from alienation. In one part of him, Leontes knows exactly what he is doing: he knows that he is creating the story as he goes along. And this is shown in the scene at the trial, when he gets the news of the death of Mamillius. The part he has aimed to play is rendered insignificant and "unreal" by the reality of his grief for his son. In a moment he casts all his disguises aside and becomes, briefly at least, an ordinary man, because a stricken father.

At some peculiar level of mental engagement he plays a game with reality.[19] For his obsession to run its course, reality must be challenged. He is not satisfied with hatching in his imagination fictitious accounts of what has happened and what will happen. He is bent on warping reality to his will. If he can do so, his fantasy life will have won out definitively and he will attain some strange dizzy height of agonized happiness. If reality cannot be so warped, the gamble *on the truth of his aspirations* will be missing, and no matter how he cheats (the disowning of the adverse Delphic message is a cheat) he will *know,* to a degree that he finds intolerable, that he is a fake.

At each round in this gruesome game one can hear the sound of desperation in the voice through the poetry—particularly in the opening stages, in Leontes' efforts to convince Camillo. To lose this round is to reduce his life to the limits of anyone else's. When he seemingly persuades Camillo to kill Polixenes, he gains his first great triumph. But when this triumph proves a defeat, and he receives the news of Camillo's flight with Polixenes, his mind readjusts itself at once to take advantage of the new event. We have in this a foretaste of the cheating we will see briefly in the denial of Delphi later.

> How blest am I
> In my just censure! in my true opinion!
> Alack, for lesser knowledge! How accurs'd
> In being so blest! There may be in the cup
> A spider steep'd, and one may drink, depart,
> And yet partake no venom (for his knowledge
> Is not infected); but if one present
> Th' abhorr'd ingredient to his eye, make known
> How he hath drunk, he cracks his gorge, his sides,
> With violent hefts. I have drunk, and seen the spider.
>
> [II, i, 36–45]

Camillo's disappearance indicates the breadth of the plot, which must necessarily be directed against him, Leontes. But in his comments at the time Leontes significantly omits any mention of his own direction to Camillo to murder Polixenes except for an allusion which is apparently not understood by his followers:

> ... that false villain,
> Whom I employ'd was pre-employ'd by him:
> He has discover'd my design, and I
> Remain a pinch'd thing; yea, a very trick
> For them to play at will.
>
> [II, i, 48–52]

That the courtiers do not understand this seems very likely, since it is only when his delusion is at an end that Leontes announces the truth as something quite new to them:

> ... recall the good Camillo,
> Whom I proclaim a man of truth, of mercy:
> For being transported by my jealousies
> To bloody thoughts and to revenge, I chose
> Camillo for the minister to poison
> My friend Polixenes.
>
> [III, ii, 156–61]

Presumably to have spoken of this earlier would have suggested a more plausible argument for Camillo's disappearance to minds other than Leontes' own. In this and other ways we can see Leontes playing catch-as-catch-can with his own suspicions.

Indeed the problem of the play, the very life of its dramatic design lies in the doubtfulness of Leontes' attitude toward reality. He is emphatically not a madman suddenly transported out of contact with the ordinary world. He is not Lear with his wits astray on the heath. He is not Ferdinand in the *Duchess of Malfi* with hallucinations poetically expressive of the terrors and wickednesses which have driven him distracted. But he is also not a man feigning that he believes suspicions which do not in fact touch him. It is rather that his jealousy is the driving force for a conflict between the value of his dreams—that is, the tortured aspirations of his fantastic life—and the reality of the life around him. This is brought out in the extraordinary interchange with Hermione at the trial.

HERMIONE

> Sir,
> You speak a language that I understand not:
> My life stands in the level of your dreams,
> Which I'll lay down.

LEONTES

> Your actions are my dreams.
> You had a bastard by Polixenes,
> And I but dream'd it!

[III, ii, 79–84]

As to the immediate meaning of this—Leontes scornfully rejects Hermione's accusation that the real peril of her life lay at the disposal of his dreams. His "dreams" are validated by her action—the birth and bastardy of Perdita. But it is plain that the verse with its strange, simple, powerful poetry is building in our minds a broader and vaguer contrast of dream and reality than is covered by Hermione's indignant charge and Leontes' sarcastic refutation, and that this indeed touches the heart of Leontes' dilemma. We are carried back to the wonderful terror of his argument with Camillo.

> Is whispering nothing?
> Is leaning cheek to cheek? is meeting noses?
> Kissing with inside lip? stopping the career
> Of laughter with a sigh (a note infallible
> Of breaking honesty)? horsing foot on foot?
> Skulking in corners? wishing clocks more swift?
> Hours, minutes? noon, midnight? and all eyes
> Blind with the pin and web, but theirs; theirs only.
> That would unseen be wicked? is this nothing?
> Why then, the world and all that's in't, is nothing,
> The covering sky is nothing, Bohemia nothing,
> My wife is nothing, nor nothing have these nothings,
> If this be nothing.

                                                    [I, ii, 284–96]

Only in the agony of the part he has imagined for himself can he find that life has any meaning at all. But the part he would play as injured husband, father, king, has its demands. He must consult his counsellors, he must stage a trial of Hermione. Yet these are only conventional acts—and indeed he has saved himself from failure ahead of time by his announcement that he does not need to follow what his counsellors say, nor be guided by their conclusions. But the approach to Delphi is an idea peculiarly his own. It is his special bout with reality, not with the outer surface of facts, the everyday happenings which in their conjunction can be construed this way or that. He will penetrate to the very center of wisdom and find out how these things— Hermione's unfaithfulness, Polixenes' plots, Camillo's treachery— *really* are, and he and his "dreams" will be vindicated!

But Leontes has also assaulted reality in another way. His course toward the vindication of the solidity and rightness of his dreams has two parts: in the one he must establish that matters were as he would have had them. He must, by the trial and by the appeal to Delphi, prove the whole plot. But he must also take positive action in his role as the injured victim who is a king. It is here he makes his great mistake. Leontes orders the child Perdita to be exposed *before* the guilt of the mother has been proved by the court and by the verdict of Delphi. It is in the interval between the arrest of Hermione and the trial, while the news from Delphi is awaited, that Leontes, raging in tortured suspense, is confronted by Paulina and the newborn baby. It is perhaps characteristic of this play that the intermediaries with the good intentions do the harm, while either sheer chance or those with nothing but interested motives produce the best results. Here Paulina, intervening bravely between her mistress and the king, only forces Leontes over the brink to direct action and brings about the exposure of the child. In the latter half of the play we are given explicitly to understand that it is the selfish desire of Camillo to see his own country again, and his readiness to betray the unfortunate young couple who trusted him that leads to the happy reconciliation. Autolycus tells us solemnly that he would not like to do a good deed as it would blot his copybook as a rogue. All the same he sends the shepherd and his son to the interested parties, Florizel and Perdita—who never think of listening to them. It is only the accidental confrontation of the shepherds and King Polixenes that produces good results.

But Leontes *has* trusted his dreams one step too far in ordering the death of Perdita. He has taken action which cannot be explained away verbally or given another face. Clearly, at some level of understanding, Leontes knew the danger of this. Hence the endless hesitation, back and forth, in the scene in which Paulina and Antigonus between them irresistibly goad him to do something decisive, and of course it is an evil thing. From this moment he has lost his fight with reality, and has made himself a criminal into the bargain.

What follows is uncanny in its dramatic re-creation of a moment which can have hardly any appropriate stage representation. Mamillius has been sick—which Leontes explains as due to his sense of his mother's dishonor. At the moment that the Delphic oracle has disowned Leontes and he makes his desperate effort to disavow Delphi, he learns that the boy is dead, and the whole pretense crumbles away. A child for a child; he has sacrificed Perdita to his dreams, and so his dreams demand the sacrifice of Mamillius. This is reality's revenge.

Mamillius has been a key figure in the dilemma of Leontes. This is the one creature that he loves more than the image he would create for himself. Hence the oddly moving half-comic scenes at the beginning between the boy and his father. The sentimental baby talk, the pretended toughness show the spot where Leontes is vulnerable. He canvasses the possibility that the boy is not his son, but this is pure acting. He never lets the idea really get near him. He not only loves and believes in the boy. He wants to have him entirely for his own. He denies him access to his mother and he interprets the boy's brokenheartedness as an agreement with his father's opinion of her. And so the death of Mamillius is for Leontes the only reality which defeats him. For it is evidence of design in the world, of real design and real retribution. This is the only thing that could have broken his hold on his dreams. With the reported death of the queen following, he is left groping for something to say or to do that will "express him truly." As the scene closes on him for the first of the three parts of the play he is fitting himself to the role of the penitent. He will mourn his wife ceaselessly day in day out with visits to the tomb, so long as his life lasts. This is the guise in which we are to find him again when we revisit Sicilia. Here and in the overt comments of the courtiers in the last act we realize that the excesses and hysteria of Leontes do not stop with the death of his son and wife. But the play does not concern itself with Leontes' second phase in anything like the detail of the first. Were it to do so, it would be a play of Leontes and this it is not. It is a play about the nature of reality—about real acts and what man's mind can do with them and what not.

Hermione's death as it is reported in Paulina's speech is one of the strangest things in Shakespeare. Nothing is left undone to deceive the audience. We are given positive assurance that she is dead, and indeed Leontes in the last act tells us that he saw her dead. She herself later tells us that she stayed alive in the hope of the recovery of Perdita as prophesied in the Delphic oracle. We have no explanation of the apparatus of this pretended death, as we do when Imogen takes the drug which puts her in a trance but will not cause death. As far as one can see, Shakespeare has wanted to deceive the audience, because in some measure it *is* Hermione's death which is needed at this point in the play. And it is (necessarily) the link with the recovery of Perdita that will recall her to life. For this the symbol of the statue—the relation of the statue to the dead-live woman—is to be used in the eventual resurrection. Shakespeare is not prepared to define the dramatic level of realism of this. He is not prepared to answer questions about Hermione's real motives for the deception, nor even exactly what Paulina is doing in it all. The important points are: Hermione is dead, as far as our knowledge and our feelings are concerned; the king will have no heir until Perdita is found; Hermione will live as a statue and come alive only when her daughter comes back, when Leontes and Hermione can see their successors, Florizel and Perdita, ready to take their places.

So far reality has figured in the play as Leontes' antagonist, defined as the player against whom his game is matched. When personalized it is Apollo, which Shakespeare has chosen to describe as the supreme non-human power. We are perhaps partly surprised when Leontes discovers in the Delphic oracle evidence of a positive judgment against him, by a god, for his wickedness. What we had expected is merely the rejection or acceptance of the oracle as an interpretation of fact. But for Leontes the sentence of the god has run upon the life of Mamillius. Here the justice of some design is made manifest, and Leontes is a criminal and must be punished.

From here on the play is indeed given over to a poetical presentation of a world where there is meaning in events. This meaning or truth emerges in the objective likelihoods inherent in the fairy story. The direction of this world does not lie with human willfulness or perversity—as it did with the fantasies of Leontes. What remains of this is the shadowy repetition of Leontes' tyranny in Polixenes' tyranny. It will be governed by a somewhat benign providence which uses preferably the worse intentions of human agents rather than the better. The scene will be lit by strange lights of irony, simple comedy, and a mysterious beauty. What the dramatic poetry will embody is the *truth* of a world animated in the fairy story.

The last outcome of Leontes' aberration, the exposure of Perdita, is the transition between the first world and the second. The tone of this scene on "the coast of Bohemia" is confusion haunted by the magnetic words of the old shepherd to his son, "Thou met'st with things dying, I with things new-born" (III, iii, 112–13). The confusion of the storm is mirrored by the confusion of the boy's description of the horrors on land and on sea —the shipwreck and the death of Antigonus. The horrors of both are suffused by the absurdity of the clown's description of the sea and the sky meeting and the bear eating the gentleman. The shepherd's comments on the hot blood and the cold body, as he looks at the baby Perdita, and on lechery and youth, are counterbalanced by the boy's muttered wish that his father had been on hand at the shipwreck where his "charity would have lacked footing." Grimness and absurdity, laughter and hate; the death of Antigonus, "pursued by a bear," is the grotesque reprisal of Apollo (presumably) for his willingness to assist in the death of the child and his final mental surrender to Leontes' slanders on Hermione. The complexion of the whole is of a confused almost comic reality which takes its place against the mental constructions of Leontes.

In the beginning of Act II young Mamillius is asked by his

mother for a tale, and he gives her a choice of one merry or sad. She chooses a merry one, but he answers, "A sad tale's best for winter" (II, i, 25). Truly enough, we get something sad for the first half of *Winter's Tale*. Later when the gentlemen of the court discuss the news of Perdita's recovery with Autolycus, one says, "This news, which is called true, is so like an old tale, that the verity of it is in strong suspicion" (V, ii, 27–29). Here the characteristics of the "old tale" are clearly the happy ending and the dovetailing of chances.[20] What the last two parts of the play are about—the scenes in Bohemia and those in Sicilia revisited—are a rendering of this strange happy ending of the "old tale" so that its verity gains support against suspicion. This is done by manipulating the reader's and audience's susceptibilities through events which reach out of the context of the story and convince us of a meaning, not completely comprehensible, indeed, but surely graceful and, to a degree, happy. The sheepshearing scene with the loving list of flowers and the puzzling description of cross-breeding; the songs of Autolycus; the statue of Hermione and its tangled associations with some plot by Hermione and Paulina—these are the pieces of stagecraft which reveal to us the world of meaning (and retribution) over which Leontes' Apollo presumably presides. "The king shall live without an heir, if that which is lost be not found" (III, ii, 134–36). All that is associated with the discovery of what is lost lives in an atmosphere exotic and shot through with ordinariness. The wildest combination of clowning (the robbery and the ballad selling) and character bits (the soliloquy of the Old Shepherd) alternate with the lyrics of Autolycus and the Arcadia of princes disguised as shepherds. It is all the time a matter of light and shade.

The conversation of Polixenes and Camillo is the tired aftermath of the Leontes story already so far removed from us by the storm and the comedy of the shepherds. Of course, Camillo is sick of Bohemia and Polixenes and wants to come home. Of course he has heard that Leontes has repented and all the emotion of those

crazy scenes so many years ago has faded. And of course Polixenes
will not let him go, and we are quite prepared for this Polixenes
to show a duplicate, if only a pale one, of Leontes—as he does
when he refuses to let his son marry a shepherd's daughter. This
is all a resumption of the first theme, a resumption that holds it in
the composition, but barely.

But the beautiful nonsense of Autolycus' song "When daffodils
begin to bloom" overwhelms it, and the comic robbery takes us
one further step away, and we are ready for Perdita and her Arcadia.[21] It is often said that these are no ordinary Arcadian scenes;
that they have the solidity of the English countryside. This is not
altogether true. The scenes need *both* the sense of artifice and
reality to have their effect. The sharp, loving distinction in the
flowers on the list is as realistic and English as can be. But no one
can take Prince Florizel and his pastoral disguise or the dance of
the shepherds as anything except a semimusical theatrical performance. It is the very element of *contrivance,* an artistic blend
of colors, that is being sought. Between the natural and artificial,
the natural countryside and the version of it which man's imaginative aspiration has created, lies the area where Perdita is, where
the hope lives that shall undo or negate the injuries of the mad
Leontes—yes, and finally also stands fresh and different against
the frenzied repentance of the father and the immobile, watchful
face of the living statue of the mother.

It is this statue that dominates the last act, in all its mystery. At
one level it becomes an ordinary sort of stage trick. There is
clearly something strange about Paulina's insistence that the king
shall not marry again—except by her permission; that, if he should
marry again it must be a choice of hers that would resemble his
former wife, as one woman was never like another. The unveiling
of the statue with the long, tantalizing stage-by-stage revelation of
the fact that Hermione has survived is rather like the proceedings
of the Duke at the end of *Measure for Measure* when he forces
Isabella to beg for the life of the man who, she supposes, has killed

her brother. We wonder here, though not perhaps very much, what sort of woman Paulina is that takes such evident pleasure in making Leontes suffer. We wonder, rather more, about Leontes' total surrender to the sense of guilt, so that there is now nothing in his life but repentance and the practice of it. Such extreme types of moral uprightness in Shakespeare are always tinted so that we are invited to comment—witness Isabella, Angelo, and the Duke himself in *Measure for Measure*. But at least as far as Paulina goes, our wonder does not rest long on her motives or actions. We are asked to accept a plot hatched by Paulina and Hermione to keep the latter in her house, alive and hidden, until her daughter should reappear. According to Hermione later, Apollo's word had convinced her of the hope of Perdita's eventual recovery. Paulina's reminders to the king of the value of his lost wife can be explained as her efforts to keep her memory alive in her husband. Her opposition to another marriage is obvious. It is hardly possible to represent this story without arousing suspicion that Paulina (and Hermione herself) are partly motivated by the wish to punish Leontes. But this is hardly of primary importance. The weight of the play does not seem to rest there. It rests on the meaning of the statue. And the first thing to realize is that strategically the device of the statue is totally unnecessary. There is no reason to suppose that Hermione has been standing like a statue for any considerable part of the sixteen years of her imprisonment. Nor can we reasonably imagine that the slow change from statue to living woman is designed to spare Leontes' weak nerves.

What we seem to have is a dramatic device expressing the inner meaning of Hermione's long absence from life and from Leontes; expressing also what the reincarnation of someone loved and thought of continually would be like, when the remembrance and the actual existence meet again, when the modifications engendered by putting a fellow being mentally into the region of the lost are jolted, when the pain and the shame of the attempted murder are suddenly brought to life and rendered factually meaningless and the dear memory and the actual extension of a living creature meet face to face. This face-to-face confrontation occurs gradually as the statue comes to life—first, the sense of likeness marred by the observed wrinkles, then the movement, then the touch and the voice. She comes to the renewal of life past as she greets the daughter, another likeness but alive and young and, alas, so like and so young that the king as he looks on her is chidden because "his eye hath too much youth in it." In Perdita he sees the contrast of the image-woman and the new reality. The gradual unveiling of the statue puts all this in its perfect histrionic setting, so that bit by bit each act calls forth its appropriate sentiment, discretely and almost embarrassingly separate from any possibility of a kindlier synthesis of emotion. The final moment of recognition falls away into silence, with the music sounding to dull our sense of too great reality and escort us to the hidden meaning of a fantasy which smiles at us enigmatically like the archaic Greek figures of the *kouroi*.

The Tempest

The two preceding plays certainly lead up to our understanding of the last—*The Tempest*. Reading the three plays in sequence is illuminating for a realization of this. Yet the closer we look, the more the last play seems to be something entirely its own.

What makes it unlike anything that went before is, above all, the magic. There was no true magic in the two other plays—even in *The Winter's Tale*. The dispositions of Apollo are supernatural, but they follow the familiar lines of the old fairy tales—of exposed children and their miraculous deliverance, the retention of their birth tokens, and their rediscovery by their parents. As to the "living statue," however strange may be its significance, we are asked to believe in it superficially at least, as the stratagem of Paulina and Hermione, hardly more fantastic than the arrangement in *Cymbeline* by which Iachimo reaches Imogen's bedroom in the trunk. Indeed it is because *The Winter's Tale* does not include magic that it strikes us as such a curious in-between world. The harshness and human clarity of Leontes' madness combines with the literary elements of the Bohemian pastoral scene, and both with the mystery of the living statue. The whole is a blend of nature and artifice. It is a Shakespearean model of a world partly as it is, partly as it might be—and the two halves reflect back and forth on each other. They are not unified by a magic through which the entire structure is subject to rules of its own. This is just what has happened in *The Tempest*. In *Winter's Tale* for the last time ordinary reality and fantasy jostle each other as separate partners. *The Tempest* is a kind of dreaming to music, represented by the magic island and Prospero its wizard, and expressed by the poetry which, wholly taking over the functions of plot and character, catches moods from the human world and turns them now topsy-turvy and now right side up. You do not enter this world as you would by the usual dramatic participation and sympathy; you listen outside and, if you are lucky, you catch the reference, though its implications are rarely very explicit.

For instance, the play conveys some sense of momentariness, the second's worth of seasonable transition from danger to safety. This is there in the broken off masque, in the suppressed impatience of Ariel. There is also the representation of some very complicated emotion in dealing with a real world which is virtually identical with the stage image of it—the fragility of both and the fragility of our understanding of them. There are Caliban and Ariel as in some sense two opposing forces controlled by or belonging to Prospero, and the latter is made to combine significantly the roles of play-producer and monarch. And generally, and most remarkably, in this play we are aware of the dissolution of the tragic mood into lyric.

But it is hard, or perhaps impossible, to relate any of these impressions or combinations of them to the whole structure of the play. It is rather a succession of moods wonderfully blended so that we discover the emotions of the real world transformed, rendered more potent than when stimulated by the sensations of ordinary life, but always removed from action and consequence—those otherwise indispensable props of dramatic emotion—and located somewhere between time and eternity.

One cannot avoid the impression everywhere of a marvelous and allusive playfulness in the author. He imposes no brake on his imagination in any need to wrestle with a difficult story, or even to be entirely comprehensible to his audience. The play is surely some sort of extended poetic commentary on many of the subjects which have lived in his head for the last ten years. But the command of his medium, the verse and the diction, has become so effortless that he can instantly and "naturally" find the exact rhythm for every nuance of feeling and thought. He lets this skill carry him into strange regions, some of them perhaps so personal as to be beyond any general explanation, sometimes to a junction of feeling and understanding where no interpretation can be more than a repetition of his own lines. Probably no one will ever find the correct explanation of why Ariel had to serve exactly the number of years he does in bondage to the witch Sycorax. Nor exactly in what sense Prospero must acknowledge Caliban as his own. But I am quite sure that no one will ever be able to relate the emotion awakened by the song "Full fadom five thy father lies;/ Of his bones are coral made" to any idea definable in terms other than the words of the song itself.

The magic has taken all the ordinary tension out of the plot. In *Cymbeline* and *Winter's Tale* we are still to some degree involved with what happens to the characters. If Imogen and Leontes are not Desdemona and Othello, their dramatic dilemmas, as patterns of action, are alive in the poetry which expresses and embodies them. But Prospero's power is so certain of success that the mainspring of our interest, the turn of events, is gone.[22] We are not much concerned for his safety, nor his deliverance from villains, nor indeed about his restoration to his rights in Milan. The working out of the love plot of Ferdinand and Miranda is perfunctory. Prospero turns from the assumed role of harsh taskmaster to that of kindly father-in-law-to-be between one scene and the next, with no more self-justification, for the former, than his confiding to us that he wants to make the love affair difficult enough to be interesting. It is only the objects before us on the stage that matter, with their strangely luminous appeal—the enchanted island, set off by the first shipwreck scene, Prospero and his two non-human associates, Ariel and Caliban, the shipwrecked visitors confronting the island's "natural" tenants.

This magic belongs to Prospero and manifests itself peculiarly on the island. And it is the possession of the magic that unites the two aspects of Prospero—the king and something else, something between wizard and dramatist.[23] As king of the island his political control is elemental; it is free of the accidents which inhere in given political situations. Both the sovereign and his subjects—momentarily to class Ariel and Caliban together—are *naturally* what they are, and their relationship a natural one. For this relationship to continue, there must be absolute control by the monarch, and only in magic is there a power which can anticipate all contingencies and prevail over all unfavorable combinations of persons and events. Prospero is a magician in this sense. He exercises royal power over Ariel and Caliban in an unqualified degree exactly as he controls the elements when he raises and allays the storm.[24]

But the island, as his realm, is hardly being presented as a commentary on commonwealths. (Indeed, it may in this regard be consciously contrasted with Gonzalo's imaginary state with its problems of government.) It is simply a place where Prospero controls *all* factors human and physical in such a way as to further his own designs. In it he can checkmate Caliban and the plot against Alonso. Once he has brought them hither, he can settle accounts from Milan days with his visitors. This island is not really a community; it is the private possession of Prospero the sorcerer who uses it, its native inhabitant Caliban, its temporary prisoner Ariel, its resources and some indefinable advantages it has for a location for his plans, to win his fight against his brother.

But it is also true that nearly the whole interest of the play centers on Prospero *on* the island. It is almost true to say that the play is about what it means to be on the island and what it means to leave it. The island is cut off from the rest of the world by the storm which ostensibly destroys the ship and its crew. (We notice also that, among her recollections of Milan, Miranda has none of how she got to the island.) A stage trick renders the effect of the storm peculiarly violent because it is not till the next scene that we know that the shipwreck has not in fact had fatal consequences. Thus there is the strongest contrast between the violence of the crew's struggles with death and the calm of the magician's study where he conducts with Miranda his protracted discussion of bygone days in Milan. This mood of detachment never leaves Prospero throughout the play. He is always contemplating what is happening—and what indeed he usually occasioned—from a great height. But it is the island which enables him to enjoy this remoteness safely. It was not so elsewhere. In Milan his bookishness—the source of his learning and ultimately his power—cost him his dukedom. Perhaps he had not yet learned enough to defend himself, but in any case he could not. On the island his studious absent-mindedness is again dangerous to his case, but on the island there is Ariel, who has taken measures against Caliban even before Prospero instructs him. And it is Ariel again who anticipates his master's orders when he frustrates the plot of Sebastian against Alonso.

It is a special moment in the story of Prospero and the island.

At hand is his vengeance on his enemies, the restoration of his rights in Milan, the betrothal of his daughter to the young prince —again the marriage of two descendants of the warring sovereigns that we know from *Winter's Tale*. Furthermore the island is for the visitors the climax of an exotic voyage stretching from Tunis to the even greater wonders here.

> Was Milan thrust from Milan that his issue
> Should become Kings of Naples? O, rejoice,
> Beyond a common joy! and set it down
> With gold on lasting pillars: in one voyage
> Did Claribel her husband find at Tunis,
> And Ferdinand, her brother, found a wife
> Where he himself was lost, Prospero his dukedom
> In a poor isle, and all of us ourselves
> When no man was his own.
>
> [V, i, 205–13]

The climax relates apparently to the island's power of inducing paradoxical self-revelation.

Prospero's power is unqualified. Ariel is wise enough to know this. It is a measure of Caliban's animal nature that he does not.[25] He learns something of this at the end of the play, though it is not certain how much. But to speak of Prospero's power in political terms, to think in the context of Shakespeare's political plays, is certainly to misread the emphasis. Power on that island is something different from the authority of a sovereign. Indeed the exercise of Prospero's rule seems almost inseparable from the art of phantom-making. Those effectual visual images which he conjures up himself or through the agency of Ariel are used both to control the course of events, which are taken dramatically to express reality, as when Ariel in the form of fire frightens the sailors from the ship, and also to entertain Ferdinand and Miranda with the masque. The end in both instances is the victory of virtue—in the correction of abuses by the good ruler and the good lessons taught by the good artist. But the achievement of the end—the

victory of virtue—seems hardly more important either to us or to
Prospero than the excitement of the strange Presences. In his own
account of the rough magic which he can practice with the aid of
the "demi-puppets" Prospero lists not only his power over the
natural forces of the world,

> [I have] 'twixt the green sea and the azur'd vault
> Set roaring war: to the dread rattling thunder
> Have I given fire, and rifted Jove's stout oak
> With his own bolt; the strong-bas'd promontory
> Have I made shake, and by the spurs pluck'd up
> The pine and cedar:

but also,

> Graves at my command
> Have wak'd their sleepers, op'd and let 'em forth
> By my so potent Art.
>
> [V, i, 43–50]

Now, sorcerers are often conceived of as raising the dead for the
entertainment of their patrons, as Faustus does. But it is not clear
for what purpose Prospero raises his "ghosts."[26] There are no patrons to give a show for. One is left with the impression that
Prospero calls the dead forth from their graves for his own delight in exercising the art. And those dead that were resurrected
may well have been the kings of the chronicle plays, to be followed by Brutus and Julius Caesar, Antony and Cleopatra.

In the masque, as in the exhibition of Prospero's power for the
control of malefactors, "our actors are all spirits." These summoned and directed by Prospero can transform the real world, re-
vive the past, ensure the safety of the future. The mystery of *The
Tempest*'s interpretation always turns on how far the specific features of the story of the wizard Duke of Milan simultaneously
express the relation of the natural ruler to his subjects and that of
the writer to the creatures of his imagination. The masque expresses the magician *formally* as a playwright. The action against

Alonso and the shipwrecked visitors, and the arranged love-making of Ferdinand and Miranda, express the magician as a controlling power in what purports to be the real world. What about the implied dimensions of Prospero's relation to Ariel and Caliban—which is really Prospero's relation to his island? For instance, Caliban certainly has a double role. He is in some sense a grotesque expression of the lowest kind of subject in the political realm. But has he some significance as the creation of the writer's mind and if so what? Is there some further dramatist's meaning in his association with the drunken clowns and the extraordinary exuberant laughter and vitality of their joint scenes?

We are constantly being reminded of the external character of Prospero's magical gifts. He is in control of his spirits when he wears his cloak—and not, when he lays it aside. At the end, with the breaking of his staff and the drowning of his book, his sorcerer's powers are ended. And at all times, except when he charms Ferdinand's sword from action, he works through his spirits—Ariel and others—and at least with the first this involves real difficulties of personal contact. Even on this wonderful island, the ordinary work tasks—the provision of food and the hauling of firewood—have to be done by someone, and someone controlled by Prospero, but also someone with special problems of treatment. The magic is very far from being entirely automatic in operation. The separability of the man and his powers tends to carry with it the sense of two distinct kinds of beings, the controller and the controlled, only nominally united for a specific purpose. In a kingdom it is easy to see that the king and his subjects are two and not one. Are the "subjects" of the playwright, his creations, separate from him? How possible is it for them to lead him where they will, make him happy, disappoint him, express truths he would rather disbelieve, disavow what he would like to accept? Shakespeare has blended this aspect of the playwright's experience with that of the monarch so that one is perpetually in doubt whether one is getting a literal version of a political ruler and his subjects or a very subtle insinuation about the work of the imagination.

As early as *Hamlet* there has been a side-by-side comparison of two kinds of controlling being—the political ruler and the dramatist. In theory the good king and the good dramatist discern what is orderly and beautiful in this world, and in their several ways help and encourage it and discourage its opposite. The king uses his wisdom and his powers of rewards and punishment to this end; in his mimic world the dramatist creates the similitude of virtue and vice and rewards them accordingly. (Incidentally, the amusement and delight the dramatist occasions by his "mirror" of nature will also aid the cause of the good and the harmonious in the world of actual events.)

In *The Tempest* both sovereigns—or rather the two aspects of the single sovereign—are seen at their most theoretical. The king is granted to be as absolute as magic can make him; the dramatic writer as free as his fancy allows. But it is the limitations that stand out. Prospero as contriver is supremely effective when it comes to storms and to masques. The physical elements do exactly what they should for him and automatically. The masque of Juno and Ceres has the pleasant univocality both in appearance and effect that attends its artificial prettiness. Its only purpose is to edify Ferdinand and Miranda by admonition, and presumably it is successful. It can be broken off before the onset of more serious business—the necessary baffling of Caliban and his fellow conspirators. This is theatricality as represented on the stage—the openly expressed want of a dimension which appears to be present in that part of the play that stands for reality.

When we turn to this *reality*, the contriver's skill appears not to be so absolute. Prospero cannot alter the nature of Sebastian and Antonio. He can only baffle their worst attempts. He cannot alter the nature of Caliban—it was a serious mistake to try and it is interesting, as a commentary on Prospero as an educative ruler, that he made the mistake. He can only drive home to Caliban the folly of rebellion against him. He cannot take from his admired assistant Ariel a preference for freedom over service with the most enlightened of masters. In all these instances, Prospero the sovereign fails against a force of nature. He can make terms, his own short-end terms, with her because of his magic. He cannot fundamentally change anything.

And this is far more so when we look at those parts of the play —Ariel, Caliban (above all Caliban), and the scenes involving the clowns on the island—which seem to have cut loose from the sketchy requirements of the formal plot and possess a quality all their own. The emphasis is certainly on material that defies the final transformation by the will of the manipulator. This defiance takes shape as an exuberance of vitality nearly monstrous, of beauty utterly beyond rational analysis, of the warmth of laughter among ugliness and cruelty. The beauty, the laughter, or the ugliness is always moving out of bounds.

Ariel's songs—his communications are nearly all songs—carry us somewhere clear of this world of sorrow, though not clear of joyful emotion. Sometimes the power they have is quite unrelated to the "meaning" of the words. Strictly speaking, "Come unto these yellow sands" is meaningless in the context of Ferdinand and his grief. Yet on us (and by implication on him) the nonsense works; it is far from being nonsense. The rhythm and even the sense of the music (which we do not have) are strong in us. We know exactly why Ferdinand says:

> Sitting on a bank
> Weeping again the King my father's wrack
> This music crept by me upon the waters,
> Allaying both their fury and my passion
> With its sweet air.

> [I, ii, 392–96]

The second song, "Full fadom five thy father lies" has pertinence, as far as words go, and anywhere else than on the island one would say very cruel pertinence, to a son's grief for a dead father. But it is not cruel here, and not only the conventional assumption of the magical power of this music on Ferdinand makes us say so. We can testify to its effect on ourselves. The nonsense of the first song with its strange wildness has carried us somewhere where we can enter into the cruel truth, "Those are pearls that were his eyes:/ Nothing of him that doth fade,/ But doth suffer a sea-change" (I, ii, 401–3), with no grief—only wonderment and joy. Ariel's instrumentality is tinged with a personal delightfulness which nonetheless always eludes any human identification as a person.

ARIEL

        Presently?

PROSPERO

        Ay, with a twink.

ARIEL

        Before you can say, "come" and "go,"
        And breathe twice, and cry, "so, so,"
        Each one, tripping on his toe,
        Will be here with mop and mow.
        Do you love me, master? no?

                        [IV, i, 41–48]

His one decisive individual intervention in the action, when he persuades Prospero, or perhaps only strengthens Prospero's inclination, to forgive the conspirators in their torment has just the right air of innocence and remoteness:

ARIEL

        Your charm so strongly works 'em,
      That if you now beheld them, your affections
      Would become tender.

PROSPERO

                Dost thou think so, spirit?

ARIEL

    Mine would, sir, were I human.

                        [V, i, 17–20]

Ariel is the spirit of lyric poetry touching tragedy and changing it. He has just enough of humanity for the task and not too much.

The concept of subject and sovereign rests lightest on the relations of Ariel and Prospero. It is, in a way, deepest on those of Prospero and Caliban. In his earthy, half-animal nature Caliban is surely Prospero's natural subject, and in his simple desire to find another monarch who would not be so hard on him, one moreover possessed of an unending store of liquor, he is something in the body politic that Shakespeare has noticed before—in *Julius Caesar* and *Coriolanus*.

But even here it is not the political identification that is at all decisive. What we have is again a stage person who enforces our sense of a reality too mixed to permit of clear analysis. We have no sure sense of what he looks like. He is apparently ugly, as befits the son of the witch Sycorax, repulsive, and half-beast. But he must be agile and quick, to judge by his own accounts of his hunting prowess. Something about him seemingly suggests a fish —perhaps this quickness and agility.[27]

The emotions he awakens are as mixed as his physical form. There is the Caliban who would have raped Miranda and delighted in Prospero's agony in seeing the island peopled with Calibans; the Caliban that urges his new master to kill Prospero, "or with a log/ Batter his skull, or paunch him with a stake,/ or cut his wezand with thy knife" (III, ii, 87–89); the Caliban of an unnatural power in malediction, "As wicked dew as e'er my mother brush'd/ With raven's feather from unwholesome fen/ Drop on you both! a south-west blow on ye/ And blister you all o'er!" (I, ii, 323–26). But there is also the Caliban who with pathos describes how first Prospero loved and "caressed" him and to whom in his blind way he offered devotion; the Caliban who tells us of the tortures which Prospero's spirit henchmen inflict upon his animal dimwittedness; the Caliban who complains— clearly with reason—that Prospero stole the island from him and, "You taught me language; and my profit on't/ Is, I know how to curse" (I, ii, 365–66); the Caliban whose strange imagination is

set to work in dreams by the island's music so that when he wakes
he "cries to dream again"; the exuberant Caliban who carries us
every step of the way with him, laughing when in his drunkenness
he sings:

> No more dams I'll make for fish;
>   Nor fetch in firing
>   At requiring;
> Nor scrape trenchering, nor wash dish:
>   'Ban, 'Ban, Ca-caliban
> Has a new master:—get a new man.
>
> [II, ii, 180–85]

And the laughter of the scene with the two-headed monster
that can drink at both ends, and the picture of the idiot conspirators stealing the finery off the clothesline after their immersion in
the filthy lake that "O'erstunk their feet"—there are dark places
being plumbed here beyond the reach of ordinary kinds of dramatic representation, perhaps beyond the reach of being given dramatic coherence in any current dramatic form. In this play Shakespeare has been drawn to the notion of a king as dramatist and a
dramatist as king arranging everything for the best, and finally
finding that only unimportant things like events can be re-
arranged. The moments which cannot be made significant in the
plot, the moods of the fairy who ostensibly acts only as an instrument of Prospero's decisions, the nature of the creature that
should be evil, clumsily absurd, whose punishment should therefore be funny and gratifying—these all turn out to be the main
source of the mysterious enchantment and bewilderment that is
the very life of the island, and of the play. They express a deeper
level of creative vitality than anything else we are watching, deeper
even than the young lovers or the king and his courtiers, deeper
perhaps than Prospero himself, who in some sense is only our
commentator and interpreter. It is here that the life of the play
rests. And these elements are in some sense beyond Prospero's
power to change or reform.

Yet it *is* Prospero who figures as our special intermediary between our world and the island, and it is through him that we
experience its elusive excitement. We are meant to share in the
evident discrepancy between the supremely successful magician,
who before our eyes has his own way in everything, and the sadness of the farewell at the end.

The play conveys a rather complete impression of Prospero as a
person. He is apparently both lonely and uneasily self-centered.
At least this seems to be the true sense of the peculiar conversation with Miranda when her father tells her the story of the old
days in Milan, before his banishment. He is constantly and petu-
lantly demanding her attention and apparently is not satisfied
with her, "Your tale, sir, would cure deafness."[28] It is much the
same in regard to Ariel. He wants his hold over Ariel to be based
on gratitude for having released him from the spells of Sycorax,
but in fact, according to himself, he finds it necessary once a
month to remind the spirit of what he has suffered. He does not
quarrel with Ariel's desire for freedom. He will miss him but
promises the reward and carries out the promise. Without believ-
ing Caliban's slander that "all the spirits do hate him as I do," we
can see that Ariel is represented as being more afraid of Prospero
than anything else. He is prepared to let Caliban's plot be far ad-
vanced rather than warn Prospero because he fears to interrupt
him at an unwelcome moment. Prospero accepts his wondering
comment on his cruelty with respect to the king and his courtiers
as a rebuke:

> Hast thou, which art but air, a touch, a feeling
> Of their afflictions, and shall not myself,
> One of their kind, that relish all as sharply
> Passion as they, be kindlier mov'd than thou art?
>
> [V, i, 21–24]

The relation with Caliban started apparently with affection on
Prospero's side and loyalty on that of Caliban, but it ended in

hatred on both. Prospero is lonely and isolated, divided from daughter and son-in-law by age and their mutual feelings, from his willing assistant, Ariel, by the difference between human and spirit, from Caliban by the difference between animal and human. He is settling his concerns for the last stage of his life.

Indeed it is one of the most remarkable effects of *The Tempest* that a play which is an uninterrupted story of success for its chief actor leaves one with the prevailing sense of melancholy and failure. The severe warning to Ferdinand and Miranda not to go to bed together before marriage, the innuendo to Sebastian and Antonio that he knows of their plot against the king and of their unchanged evil, the sadness of the comment on Miranda's "O brave new world," and the final "and thence retire me to my Milan, where/ Every third thought shall be my grave"—certainly make one feel that Prospero's drive and vitality, which enabled him to plan and carry out the defeat of his foes and the requisite new start for the future, expired with that moment in the play when these results were formally achieved. What is left is the weariness of an old man who has no longer any passionate concern even with what is good and right in the new pattern of events to which he has lent his help. The doubleness of life in beauty and ugliness, the imperfection of consummation, the frailty of humanity, the terror of death's meaninglessness, are too much for him—as a person. And we have really only entered into this story through his person. It is not exactly that we care about what happens to him. But it is his vision that has shown us everything in the play, and as he grows weary and ready for death, we enter into his mood. Prospero has been just enough of a character to permit us to do this—to maintain a sensitive connection with the poetic image of the world created in the rest of the play, while accepting, at almost a naturalistic level of sympathy, the truth of the old man's sadness.

For Prospero's farewell to life is not the usual farewell of someone on the threshold of death. The end of his life in Milan is only one aspect, and for us and him the least important, of the unhappy finality of the end. It is goodbye to the island, goodbye to Ariel, goodbye maybe even to the dimension of life involved in the relation with Caliban. Above all, the farewell is haunted by the confused emotion of the equation of the theater and reality. As the stage scenery comes down, and the spirits that have enacted the roles vanish, so do the towers and palaces of the real world and the men, including himself, "and the great globe itself" fade into nothingness. The end of the masque connects with the end of the stay on the island and the end of life. Only Ferdinand can dream of living on the island forever. It is apparently as impossible to live there forever as it is to live anywhere else forever. But it has also some other added element of impossibility. One is forced to give the island up by something in oneself, before actual death seizes the mortal being. And here is the real sharpness of parting.

What is constantly being asserted in *The Tempest,* in each renewed complicated assault on our emotions, is the richness, both for good and bad, of life on the island. It is humanity's experience enriched and intensified by powers that humans do not possess. Prospero can revenge himself, redress wrongs, prevent others in the making, even enjoy the generosity of forgiveness without risk, because he has won completely.

But it is also a quality of the play to make us feel the contrast between the enrichment of life on the island and the very magical powers which at first seem to constitute that enrichment. Prospero remains human. He is still faced with the finiteness of life and its symptoms—his remotion from others, the sad superiority of his experience, the true discovery of universal fragility. And not only is he human in facing death. He remains human in his demands in life—despite his magic. The two necessary elements of his continued existence on the island remain unassailably separated from him, to his sorrow. Caliban escaped love and reformation through his underlying implacable earthiness. Ariel's irresponsible beauty cannot be tamed to an indefinite willing association. Because Prospero is human, he cannot be contented with power; he wants the love and support of assistants proffered willingly and forever. That cannot be. There is no forever, and beings so different from him cannot see a meaning in their relationship. So, in a certain sense, the magic that enriches the island can also be separated from it. It can be seen as a factor in the situation. It is indeed the *light* that enables us to see life on the island in a new way, and to understand things otherwise beyond our comprehension.

The task of revenge for the wrongs committed in Milan has disguised from us (and perhaps we are meant to think from Prospero too) the truth that the exercise of the magic is more exciting than the ends for which it is exercised. In this play we are seeing the moment which is the end of a long apprenticeship. Presumably the bookish Prospero of early Milan days was seeking for occult knowledge, like Faustus. But he had hardly attained any great proficiency, yet, or the conspirators who bundled him and Miranda out so unceremoniously would not have had so easy a task. He has come far since then, and this has demanded a lot of study and a lot of practice. When he dwells with delight on his feats in causing natural eruptions (with the aid of the "demi-puppets") and summoning the dead from their graves, there is no reason to think that these feats are undertaken in the course of any direct prosecution of his designs on restoration. Here he is practicing, presumably against the day when he would use it for this purpose, to win back his own. But clearly, from the speech, the practice was itself a joy. The purpose has been accomplished. There is nothing left but to retire from what now appears to have been only a scene peculiarly suited to the special powers necessary for his successful vengeance.[29]

But here what the play has said to the audience is something different from the simple story of Prospero's success. The *island itself* has become for us some peculiar and unique expression of humanity's experience, not only intensified but ambiguously altered. We float between the musical enchantment of Ariel's songs and the dark, sensual, comic genius of Caliban; between the rights and wrongs of the latter and some hint of a realm where there is a new concept of rule; between the laughter and clowning of the three, Trinculo, Stephano, and Caliban, and the rarefied courtship of Ferdinand and Miranda. Perhaps we feel ourselves on the brink of a new reality. This is what the island *is* for us, and that is the deepest reason for our sympathetic emotion when Prospero takes his leave of it.

The island is not the theater. It is the dimension in which is expressed the playwright's reality when he has created it—and in this play largely *while* he is creating it, while it is emerging from him only partly sprung of his conscious intention and craftsmanship. The island has been Prospero's as Milan never was and never will be. The only creature that has any justifiable claim against him in its ownership is also in some sense *his*—whatever that may mean. Ariel was always more separated as a being; it was the contract of obligation alone that bound him. The life on the island and the happenings there express the process of creation for the writer; they also express something new that he found himself creating—something really new that altered all the previous guidelines. Either he could not see his way further or for some reason he was disinclined to travel it. But he knew that he was leaving his new world unexplored. The fairy music brings us too to the edge of the unknown. There are echoes of older melodies that we catch but it is the full volume of the new strain that we long to hear—vainly.

Notes

1. Fletcher wrote, "A tragi-comedy is not so called in respect of mirth and killing, but in respect it wants deaths, which is enough to make it no tragedy, yet brings some near it which is enough to make it no comedy,

which must be a representation of familiar people, with such kind of trouble as no life shall be questioned. . . ."

2. For a discussion of the history and nature of tragicomedy see A. H. Thorndike, *The Influence of Beaumont and Fletcher on Shakespere,* pp. 115–19, 134, 136–37.

Ellis-Fermor is inclined to underplay Shakespeare's debt to the younger dramatists: "By one of those paradoxes which this drama continually offers us, Shakespeare used for the culminating expression of his faith in reality that form which its inventors had devised as a means of escape. The fairy-tale with him becomes charged with those implications which the more immediate types of story could not present, becomes the vehicle of imaginative experience and interprets the real world more truly than do the records of actuality" (Una Ellis-Fermor, *The Jacobean Drama,* p. 268).

3. All quotations from these plays are drawn from the new Arden Shakespeare editions (Cambridge: Harvard University Press), Una Ellis-Fermor, Harold F. Brooks, and Harold Jenkins, general editors: *Cymbeline,* ed. J. M. Nosworthy (1955); *The Winter's Tale,* ed. J. H. P. Pafford (1963); *The Tempest,* ed. Frank Kermode (1954).

4. J. M. Nosworthy citing Pettet's *Shakespeare and the Romance Tradition* argues that this combining of elements is appropriate to romance literature. *Cymbeline* and *Pericles* are experimental attempts to adapt this tradition to the stage. But only in *Winter's Tale* and *The Tempest* does he think the adaptation successful (*Cymbeline,* pp. xlvii–lii).

Tillyard thinks one of the major characteristics of the last plays is the juxtaposition of different "planes of reality" (E. M. W. Tillyard, *Shakespeare's Last Plays,* pp. 59 ff.).

Quiller-Couch explains the confusion in these plays rather more technically. Shakespeare, he thinks, wanted to deal with a new theme (reconciliation, forgiveness) which was not particularly well suited to the stage (Sir Arthur Quiller-Couch, *Notes on Shakespeare's Workmanship,* pp. 205–8, 301–4, and *passim.*

5. F. R. Leavis ("Criticism of Shakespeare's Last Plays: A Caveat," *Scrutiny,* 10 [1941]: 341) remarks, "The relations between character, speech and the main themes of the drama are not such as to invite a psychologizing approach. . . . The personal drama is made to move upon a complexity of larger rhythms—maturity, death, birth. . . . Spring, Summer, Winter, Spring."

See also: F. C. Tinkler, "Cymbeline," *Scrutiny,* 7 (1938): 5–19; A. A. Stephenson, S.J., "The Significance of 'Cymbeline,'" *Scrutiny,* 10 (1942): 329–38; Derek Traversi, *Shakespeare: The Last Phase;* John Middleton Murry, *Shakespeare,* pp. 326–38; Caroline F. E. Spurgeon, *Shakespeare's Imagery.*

6. The tragic pattern, Tillyard thinks (*Shakespeare's Last Plays*), involves, as a last step after prosperity and its destruction, some sort of recon-

ciliation or regeneration (p. 16). The great tragedies only hint at this (pp. 17–18); the last plays focus on it entirely. "In them the old order is destroyed as thoroughly as in the main group of tragedies" (p. 25). See also J. Dover Wilson, *The Essential Shakespeare*, pp. 140–41.

7. Strachey explained the mood of the last plays by saying of Shakespeare: "Is it not thus, then, that we should imagine him in the last years of his life? Half enchanted by visions of beauty and loveliness, and half bored to death; on the one side inspired by a soaring fancy to the singing of ethereal songs, and on the other urged by a general disgust to burst occasionally through his torpor into bitter and violent speech? If we are to learn anything of his mind from his last works, it is surely this" (Lytton Strachey, "Shakespeare's Final Period" in *Books and Characters*, p. 60; the essay was first published in 1906). Strachey's statement was a reaction against nineteenth-century critics such as Swinburne, Furnivall, ten Brink, Gollancz, Sidney Lee, Brandes, and above all Dowden, who thought that in this last period, Shakespeare had reached a state of quiet serenity and peace with the world (Edward Dowden, *Shakspere*, pp. 55, 60).

8. A. C. Bradley said (*Shakespearean Tragedy*, p. 27), "Dramas like *Cymbeline* and the *Winter's Tale*, which might seem destined to end tragically, but actually and otherwise, owe their happy ending largely to the fact that the principal characters fail to reach tragic dimension. And conversely, if these persons were put in the place of the tragic heroes, the dramas in which they appeared would cease to be tragedies.

Similarly, Leavis remarks ("Shakespeare's Last Plays," p. 342) that Posthumus is like Othello of romantic convention.

9. Granville-Barker, who agrees in substance with my portrait of Cloten, thinks these speeches give him a "sort of dignity" and show him as a soldier and gentleman (Harley Granville-Barker, "Cymbeline" in *Prefaces to Shakespeare*, pp. 321–25).

10. See *ibid.*, pp. 305–21.

11. Nosworthy (*Cymbeline*, pp. lix–lx) thinks Posthumus a "tragically debased" figure and is not persuaded by his speech of repentance. Also see Granville-Barker, "Cymbeline," p. 327.

12. Shaw thought there were two Imogens, one "fertile and spontaneous in nasty ideas . . . the other an enchanting person of delicate sensitiveness" (from a letter to Miss Ellen Terry quoted in G. B. Shaw, *Shaw on Shakespeare*, p. 56).

13. Both Nosworthy (*Cymbeline*, p. lv) and Granville-Barker ("Cymbeline," p. 257) think the contriving of Cloten's decapitation makes his death less horrible.

14. Traditionally, it has been claimed that the sources are Holinshed (the story of Cymbeline and the Roman invasion) and the *Decameron*, ninth story, second day (Imogen and Posthumus). The story of Belarius and the king's two sons seems substantially of Shakespeare's own invention (though

it too may in part derive from Holinshed). A number of variations of the Boccaccio story have also been suggested, most notably *Westward for Smelts* (which Nosworthy discounts) and *Fredryke of Jennen* (which he supports). The sons are mentioned by name in *The Faerie Queene* and *A Mirror for Magistrates*. Nosworthy thinks the main source was a romantic drama, *Love and Fortune* (1582). Sources are discussed and reprinted at length in Nosworthy, *Cymbeline,* pp. xvii–xxviii, 197–216; H. H. Furness, ed., *Cymbeline,* in *The Variorum Shakespeare,* pp. 455–481; and *Holinshed's Chronicle as Used in Shakespeare's Plays,* ed. Allardyce and Josephine Nicoll, pp. 228–33.

15. Earlier critics, according to Furness (*Cymbeline,* p. xiv), "extolled the marvellous dramatic skill" of the denouement.

16. Granville-Barker ("Cymbeline," pp. 237 ff.) describes the play as artless but says, ". . . it is obviously a sophisticated, not a native artlessness, the art that rather displays art than conceals it" (p. 243).

17. George Orwell, "England Your England" in *A Collection of Essays* (Garden City: Doubleday Anchor Books, 1954), p. 260.

18. J. H. P. Pafford observes that Shakespeare labored to make the plot of the play much more plausible than that of its source, *Pandosto,* a novel by Robert Greene (Pafford, ed., *Winter's Tale,* pp. lxiv–lxvii). The source is reprinted and discussed, *ibid.* pp. xxvii– xxxvii, 181–225, and in H. H. Furness, ed., *The Winter's Tale* in *The Variorum Shakespeare,* pp. 321–52.

19. A number of critics have suggested that the main theme of the play is the power of art and imagination. But they limit their discussion to the scene between Polixenes and Perdita and to the statue scene, and are content to say that imagination brings good out of evil. They fail to take account of the negative powers of imagination shown in Leontes. See, for example, Murry, *Shakespeare,* pp. 326 ff.; Derek Traversi, "The Winter's Tale" in *Shakespeare: The Comedies,* ed. Kenneth Muir (Englewood Cliffs: Prentice-Hall, 1965), pp. 157–60 and *passim.*

20. See also Paulina's remark (V, iii, 115–17):

> That she is living,
> Were it but told you, should be hooted at
> Like an old tale: but it appears she lives.

21. Traversi, "The Winter's Tale," pp. 153–54 and *passim.*

22. For agreement with the substance of this statement (but with a very different interpretation) see E. E. Stoll, *Shakespeare's Young Lovers,* pp. 106–7: "When two souls are wholly pure and simple, all barriers . . . either lacking or burned away—when there is no longer pretence or deception, nor even, as ordinarily in Shakespeare, a disguise or a play of wits—then, as here in *The Tempest,* there is little place left for drama. Extremes . . . often meet, high romantic spirits surrender to each other (though with what a difference!) as simply and completely as the silly and the irresponsible—and then, as Shakespeare seems to have recognized, the dramatist's occupation's gone."

23. For a brief explanation of contemporary attitudes toward enchanters

and fairies, see Dr. Johnson's introduction in *Johnson on Shakespeare,* pp. 64–66.

24. For other implications inherent in this position see, for instance, A. C. Bradley, "The tendency which . . . produced Ariel and Caliban [is] the tendency of imagination to analyse and abstract, to decompose human nature into its constituent factors, and then to construct beings in whom one or more of these factors is absent or atrophied or only incipient" (*Shakespearean Tragedy,* p. 212).

25. Traversi ("The Tempest," *Scrutiny,* 16 [1949]) argues, "[The words] 'nobly' and 'rich' become clearly associated with the vision of a redeemed ennobled humanity and with the new vitality that springs from the harmonizing of the passions" (pp. 149 ff.). He later connects nobility with reason (p. 153). Prospero's power lies in his ability to judge—and judgment can take place only when good and evil in human nature are separated and understood (p. 148). Thus Caliban would be innately incapable of realizing the nature of Prospero's power. See also Kermode, *The Tempest,* pp. liv–lix.

26. Various editors have pointed out the echo of Ovid's *Metamorphosis* V. i. 33–50, which includes also the raising of the dead, "manesque exire sepulcris."

27. Caliban may have appeared less strange to an Elizabethan audience than he does to us. After Malone, most commentators have agreed that the sources of *The Tempest,* such as they are, were pamphlets concerning the wreck of Sir George Somers and Sir Thos. Gates on Bermuda. See Edmond Malone, *An Account of the Incidents from Which the Title and Part of the Story of Shakespeare's Tempest Were Derived;* Rudyard Kipling, *How Shakespeare Came To Write the Tempest;* Kermode, *The Tempest,* pp. xxvi–xxxiv, 135–41; Furness, *The Tempest* in *The Variorum Shakespeare,* pp. 306–51.

Daniel Wilson (*Caliban: The Missing Link*) points out that numerous travelers (Mandeville and Polo for example) had made familiar "the idea of beings monstrous and brutal in every physical characteristic, and yet in some not clearly defined sense, human" (pp. 14–15). "The new world . . . seemed more fitly occupied by Calibans than any ordinary type of humanity" (pp. 44–45, 70–71). A few Indians had been brought to London from the New World and had attracted much attention. See Trinculo's speech (II, ii, 28–34).

28. Traversi thinks that the end of the play is reconciliation and that judgment (between good and evil) is the precondition of reconciliation. He therefore argues that Prospero is insisting Miranda learn judgment, "awakening her into maturity" by this piece of instruction ("The Tempest," pp. 128–29).

29. Most critics feel totally different about this. See Bradley, *Shakespearean Tragedy,* p. 263; J. Dover Wilson, *The Essential Shakespeare,* p. 143, and *The Meaning of the Tempest,* pp. 21–23; Murry, *Shakespeare,* pp. 332–33; G. Wilson Knight, *Myth and Miracle,* p. 27.

SELECTED BIBLIOGRAPHY

Bethel, S. L. *The Winter's Tale: A Study*. New York: Staples Press, 1947.

Bradley, A. C. *Shakespearean Tragedy*. New York: Meridian Books, 1963.

Brandes, Georg. *William Shakespeare*. New York: Macmillan, 1899.

Chambers, Sir Edmund K. *Shakespeare: A Survey*. London: Sidgwick and Jackson, 1925.

————. *William Shakespeare: A Study of Facts and Problems*. 2 vols. Oxford: Clarendon Press, 1930.

Coleridge, Samuel Taylor. *Shakespearean Criticism*. 2 vols. Everyman's Library. New York: Dutton, 1964.

Dowden, Edward. *Shakspere*. Literature Primers. New York: American Book Co., n.d.

Ellis-Fermor, Una. *The Jacobean Drama*. London: Methuen & Co., 1958.

Furness, Horace H., ed. *A New Variorum Edition of Shakespeare*. Vol. IX, *The Tempest;* Vol. XI, *The Winter's Tale;* Vol. XVIII, *Cymbeline*. Philadelphia: Lippincott, 1892, 1898, 1913.

Granville-Barker, Harley. *Prefaces to Shakespeare*. 2d series. London: Sidgwick and Jackson, 1939.

Holinshed, Raphael. *Holinshed's Chronicle as Used in Shakespeare's Plays*. Edited by Allardyce and Josephine Nicoll. Everyman's Library. New York: Dutton, 1965.

Johnson, Samuel. *Johnson on Shakespeare*. London: Humphrey Milford, Oxford University Press, 1929.

Kermode, Frank, ed. *The Tempest*. Vol. 6 in *The (New) Arden Shakespeare*. Cambridge: Harvard University Press, 1954.

Kipling, Rudyard. *How Shakespeare Came To Write the Tempest*. New York: Dramatic Museum of Columbia University, 1916.

Knight, G. Wilson. *Myth and Miracle*. London: E. J. Burrow & Co., 1929.

————. *The Shakespearean Tempest*. London: Oxford University Press, 1932.

Kott, Jan. *Shakespeare, Our Contemporary*. Translated by Bronislaw Taborski. Garden City: Doubleday, 1964.

Leavis, F. R. "Criticism of Shakespeare's Last Plays: A Caveat," *Scrutiny*, 10 (1941).

Malone, Edmond. *An Account of the Incidents from Which the Title and Part of the Story of Shakespeare's Tempest Were Derived*. London: C. & R. Baldwin, 1808.

Murry, John Middleton. *Shakespeare*. New York: Harcourt, Brace & Co., 1936.

Northam, John R. *Dividing Worlds*. New York: Humanities Press, 1965.

Nosworthy, J. M., ed. *Cymbeline*. Vol. 6 in *The (New) Arden Shakespeare*. Cambridge: Harvard University Press, 1955.

Pafford, J. H. P., ed. *The Winter's Tale*. Vol. 23 in *The (New) Arden Shakespeare*. Cambridge:

Harvard University Press, 1963.

Pettet, E. C. *Shakespeare and the Romance Tradition.* New York: Staples Press, 1949.

Quiller-Couch, Sir Arthur. *Notes on Shakespeare's Workmanship.* New York: Henry Holt, 1917.

Shaw, G. B. *Shaw on Shakespeare.* Edited by Edwin Wilson. New York: E. P. Dutton, 1961.

Spurgeon, Caroline F. E. *Shakespeare's Imagery.* New York: Macmillan, 1936.

Stephenson, A. A., S.J. "The Significance of 'Cymbeline,'" *Scrutiny,* 10 (1942).

Still, Colin. *Shakespeare's Mystery Play.* London: Cecil Palmer, 1921.

Stoll, E. E. *Shakespeare and Other Masters.* Cambridge: Harvard University Press, 1940.

———. *Shakespeare's Young Lovers.* London: Oxford University Press, 1937.

Strachey, Lytton. "Shakespeare's Final Period," in *Books and Char-* *acters.* London: Chatto and Windus, 1922.

Thorndike, A. H. *The Influence of Beaumont and Fletcher on Shakespeare.* New York: Ams Press, 1966.

Tillyard, E. M. W. *Shakespeare's Last Plays.* London: Chatto and Windus, 1938.

Tinkler, F. C. "Cymbeline," *Scrutiny,* 7 (1938).

Traversi, Derek. *Shakespeare: The Last Phase.* Stanford: Stanford University Press, 1965.

Wain, John. *The Living World of Shakespeare.* London: Macmillan, 1964.

Wilson, Daniel. *Caliban, the Missing Link.* London: Macmillan, 1873.

Wilson, J. Dover. *The Essential Shakespeare.* Cambridge: Cambridge University Press, 1932.

———. *The Meaning of "The Tempest."* The Literary and Philosophical Society of Newcastle upon Tyne, 1936.

Sophocles

INTRODUCTION

There are three plays of Sophocles which deal, roughly speaking, with a common theme. Two, *Philoctetes* and *Oedipus at Colonus,* were written within the last five years of his long life, that is, between 409 and 405 B.C.; one, *Ajax,* was written many years earlier, probably in 442. Of course to group the three together destroys the seemingly more natural links that exist between the two plays called after Oedipus and that which deals with the later stage of the legend, *Antigone.* There certainly is a fairly coherent interpretation of the whole legend which Sophocles entertained and expressed in the three plays, *Oedipus the King, Oedipus at Colonus,* and *Antigone.* But *Antigone* was written in the 440's, sometime about the date of *Ajax, Oedipus the King* about 427, and *Oedipus at Colonus* appeared posthumously. However much the revisiting of the Oedipus legend indicates the playwright's interest, it is also clear to anyone who reads *Philoctetes* and *Oedipus at Colonus* in quick succession that these two plays, composed within a few years of each other, have much in common and that the situation described is sufficiently similar so that the author's imagination is evidently working on the same idea. Philoctetes and Oedipus, although embedded in different legends, are expressive of the same dilemma. Both are outcasts from their communities, and loaded with suffering and bitterness. Both are burdened with afflictions which make for instinctive aversion and disgust wherever they come. There is a suggestive relationship between the infected foot and the stain of parricide and incest. In both men there is hidden a magical potency, discovered at last by those who cast them out, which leads to an act of restoration or restitution for the previous rejection.

In both plays the dramatic emphasis is inclined to rest on the feelings of the man who becomes aware of his change in value, from a creature universally abhorred to an object of honor. Each of the characteristic phases of his life has been assigned to the hero for no sensible human reason, by some incomprehensible divinity. The pains or pleasures of his lot have been disposed of by fellow men who act unhesitatingly in obedience to the god's orders. They expel him or restore him apparently without any feeling of fellowship with the victim. It is true that the two plays suggest that in certain circumstances the portentous man, now cursed, now blessed by God, may find, among his own kind, friendship and charity of a different sort. But in general people are inclined to treat him strictly according to what is in it for themselves. Surely these two plays present aspects of the hero and his situation which are conceived in common. The variations belong to the individual vitality of the legendary figures of Philoctetes and Oedipus.

We will never know what connections exit between this subject and the last years of the old Sophocles. But we can see, if we look at *Ajax,* written more than thirty years earlier than *Philoctetes,* that in embryo many of the same ideas and, fundamentally, the same plot are there in the older play. This is not obvious at once because *Ajax,* as Sophocles wrote it, does not make explicit the final act of the story, the elevation of the criminal to the status of the community's benefactor and protector. Instead, the end of the play is concerned with Ajax' right to burial. Now the burial, though demanded for Ajax on general religious grounds, is urged by Odysseus with an important addition. He says to Agamemnon: "You will not destroy him [Ajax] by denying him burial, but the ordinances of the gods; and moreover it is not just to injure *the good man* if he dies, no matter how you may hate him" (ll. 1342–45). That is, the act of burial is a token that the community has balanced his former services against his recent crime and allowed him due credit for the former against the latter.

The theme of the right of the dead to burial in a play so close in time to *Antigone* seems almost to make *Ajax* another statement of *Antigone*. But to the Athenian audience the decision to accord burial, or rather the fight to avert the ignominy of refusing it, is linked with the significance of the cult of Ajax of Salamis, the hero who was thought to have fought on Athens' side against Persia in the battle which took place by his island sanctuary.[1] Thus the vindication of the savior-hero is involved in his winning of the right of burial. As soon as we remember this, it is plain that the significance of the story is much the same as in *Philoctetes* and *Oedipus at Colonus*. All three deal with the ambiguous figure of the outlaw who is later chosen by the gods to be the community's protector; all three treat, at least by implication, the ambiguity of the relation of divine command to human implementation of the command; all three show the isolation of this special kind of hero, if we think of him as such, from association with his own kind; all three are concerned, if incidentally, with the relation of the time process to the original act, with the possibility or impossibility of restitution or retribution.

The dramatic problem of the plays centers in the character of the suffering hero and his destiny. His reinstatement in power, as arbitrarily enjoined by the gods as his original destruction, is attained only after his death or symbolic death. It seems as though the man in possession of his new power—the magic of Oedipus' tomb, the invincibility of the healed Philocetetes and his bow, the hero status of Ajax of Salamis—must be as much outside the community in its final transformation as the man was during his years of isolation and banishment. Yet both the isolation and the later position of power exist with relation to the community—to that of Greece or Athens. It is hardly the exaltation of the hero as an individual man with which the play is concerned.

This is not the view ordinarily taken of these plays, especially of *Ajax* and *Philoctetes,* and apparently with reason. It is true that in this story of the hero first cursed and then blessed by the non-human powers of the world Sophocles has concentrated his attention neither on the occasion of the original curse nor on the final elevation of the hero but principally on the suffering in between and on the hero's bearing of it. As a result most of the more recent critics try to show that the dramatist has stressed those qualities in the suffering *man* which make sense of the union of antecedent sinner and subsequent hero. Thus a kind of Sophoclean theology is constructed into which the suffering and the elevation of the hero fit. For instance there is C. Whitman, who does not restrict his characterization of the hero in Sophocles to those plays I have chosen but regards a broader version of it as typical. He speaks of Sophocles as the dramatist of a new idea of "heroic humanism." This "heroic humanism" is the assumption by man of heroic attributes earlier conceived of as exclusively divine, and the attribution of typical evil (such as Ajax' madness) to some supernatural forces, to some sort of gods, though these too are not exactly the powers of the old fashioned Olympian hierarchy. He speaks of the play *Ajax* as follows: "Rather, if the whole be taken as meaning more than the part, the *Ajax* reveals itself as one long paean of triumphant individualism."[2]

Now, curiously enough, it is exactly the heroic individual that does not triumph in these three plays. Ajax dies without friends or follower, throwing away his own life in pure misery. It is in his burial, in the vindication of his honorable status, that the triumph resides, if anywhere. It is surely on this, and on the acknowledgment by Odysseus that all men, as well as Ajax, can be destroyed by the gods, that the dramatic emphasis rests. It is much the same in *Philoctetes* and *Oedipus at Colonus*. Philoctetes is forced to surrender his human sense of injury and his desire for revenge and must serve the cause of his enemies in order to fulfill the destiny imposed on him by the god. Oedipus is finally in a position to gratify his hatred of Creon and his own sons but only when he is already almost "nothing" as he says himself.

OEDIPUS

When I am no longer anything, am I a man?

ISMENE

Yes, for now the gods raise you up, then they destroyed you.

OEDIPUS

It is a poor thing to raise up the old man that fell when young.

[*Oedipus at Colonus,* ll. 393–95]

He has to struggle to prevent his grave from becoming an advantage to his foes, so completely will the personality of his ghost-spirit cease to have connections with his present self. It does not seem possible, in the light of these plays, to claim that Sophocles is presenting a triumph of heroic humanism or the heroic individual as such.

Yet certainly the direction of attention in such critics as Whitman is right. If it is not the "heroic humanism" of these peculiar sinners that is being celebrated, something new and strange *is* being asserted by Sophocles about the relation of these men and the divine, and about the ethical and moral values which the men represent. It cannot be that Sophocles has presented the vividness of suffering of Ajax, Philoctetes, and Oedipus and empha-sized the special role of these heroes without implying the kind of tragic universe in which they find their dishonor and redemp-tion. This is surely a kind of theology. Let us try to suggest it, in outline, and then give it content by examining the particular plays.

The tragic universe of the three plays is one where the dyna-mism of the outcast hero is an integral part of the cosmic design. Man's social unit, the state, cannot continue to exist without this dynamism. The power of the hero is a kind of natural force and as such is never adequately judged or expressed by men's notions of moral excellence. Only an inadequate and incomplete relation exists between their ethical values and the heroic power. For the final emergence of this power the destruction of the human, the purely human, personality is necessary. This is not purification by suffering; it is not the same man purified that survives. That man has perished, physically in Ajax, morally, I believe, in Philoctetes, and totally except for his posthumous heroic status in Oedipus.

It is as a vindication of something different that we must see his final success, if we think of it as such. We may finally come to feel that the human terms in which we judge good and bad are not truly matched with the stories of these heroes. For the bad qualities which his fellows attribute to the suffering hero are genuinely there. Ajax is arrogant and Philoctetes full of hate and suspicion, Oedipus unjust and cruel. These are not to be seen as virtues, for this is to pervert our normal human standards. They are not for imitation by ordinary good-or-bad people who quite sensibly blame the heroes for acting as they do. But their bad qualities, as expressed by the dramatist, are the diagnostic marks of the hero who is later translated. For he has been placed in a position such that he *must* sin against ordinary human standards of good sense and morality in resenting the gods' treatment of him and in particular in resenting the way in which the community has implemented the divine command. The strength of the plays lies in their rendering of what it feels like to be this hero, caught between the gods and men. One aspect of the interpretation bears on the mysterious meaning of the community in relation to its greatest men, those unpolitical ones that are either beasts or gods. There is an expression here histrionically of moral values which are not entirely translatable into human moral values, because there is for Sophocles a split between those that man rationally accepts for society, or regards as the safest basis for the relations of man and the divine, and on the other hand those values that belong to the dynamic of the spiritual universe.

Ajax

There are three main difficulties in finding a satisfactory meaning for *Ajax* and they are all concerned with the unity of the play— unity in construction and characterization. The first and biggest question is, What are we to make of the broken-backed plot? Ajax commits suicide two-thirds of the way through the play, and the rest deals with the issue of his burial. What is the design of the whole such that we lose the central figure so early (and with such a dramatic finale) and are left with Teucer's quarrel with the Atreidae and the unexpected support of Odysseus to conclude the piece?[3] There is really no parallel to this in the other plays of Sophocles.

The second crux is how to interpret the speech of repentance which Ajax utters before going away to kill himself. Is this a deception of Tecmessa and his friends to blind them to his intentions? Or is it a genuine recantation of his whole attitude, related to his earlier sins of hybris?

The final ambiguity concerns the death itself. We are told in the herald's speech that Athena will have her power over him for only twenty-four hours. If he can be kept in his tent for that time he may escape; but if he goes out during this period it will be the end of him. Ajax does go out, and kills himself by the seashore. Now, is this the final punishment by Athena—that is, does she drive him out of his wits again and so bring him to kill himself? (This is how C. M. Bowra reads it.)[4] In that case surely the emphasis of the play lies from beginning to end in the relation of Ajax and Athena and the issue of the hero's hybris. This would fit with the interpretation of the repentance speech as genuinely expressing Ajax' new feelings. Ironically, Athena would kill him just after she had broken his resolution.

But a very serious obstacle to understanding the play in this way is that there is no sensible explanation of the importance Sophocles has given to the issue of burial. In some sense the latter is clearly a rehabilitation. At the very least, it sets a limit to the punishment that the early authorities can exact for his fault. Why? If the goddess is punishing a guilty man for his insolence, why does the play in its end stress the victory of some aspect of the man's goodness?

Now suppose that the death of Ajax is not to be understood merely as the final act of Athena's vengeance. Suppose that Ajax kills himself as a final act of defiance of this world, the gods that govern it, and the men that administer the community under their government;[5] suppose that the speech of repentance is indeed a piece of deception, as Tecmessa herself afterwards thinks it is, and that what truth there is in it is simply Ajax' confession that the world and he cannot get on together any longer and that he must either submit or die—with the suppressed conclusion that he prefers to die. Then we must understand the final act involving Teucer's defense of his brother and Odysseus' commentary on his right to burial in a new light. This must in fact be a play in which Ajax the humiliated hero represents some value that is finally triumphant, in which the punishment by Athena is not the single or perhaps the most important judgment on Ajax the man or the representative of something between man and god.

The presentation of Ajax' crime, and Ajax as a criminal within the play's scope, has already something curious about it. The tendency appears to be throughout to bear lightly on the most serious aspects of his offense. We see him first when the crime has already been committed. (This is incidentally also true of *Philoctetes* and *Oedipus at Colonus*.) We see not the act itself but the suffering that follows it. We see the confrontation of the crazy Ajax and the goddess who blinds his eyes and his mind. We see his humiliation, all the more remarkable because he himself is as yet unaware of it, being exhibited for his enemy Odysseus. There seems to be only one emotion that the dramatist wishes us to experience—pity. Pity for the destruction of the hero and the heroic personality, reinforced by fear because, as Odysseus says, "Everything may happen when a god contrives." He or any other fortunate man may at any moment find himself in Ajax' place.

This pity, as the play goes on, is powerfully reinforced by the sense of the lost grandeur of the man, by his sheer capacity for suffering, and his shame. Also by his loneliness. He is too roughly masculine and too inhibited to welcome Tecmessa's affection and sympathy though he may well be correctly interpreted as understanding it. His brother, his only intimate, is absent. He sees himself netted around by enemies. His act of shame in killing the cattle and the herdsmen will cause nothing but laughter, while it affords pretext for punishing him. His suicide he can imagine greeted by exactly the comment Menelaus makes, "We had difficulty enough with him in life; at least we will manage him dead" (ll. 1067–68).

The size of Ajax remains impressed on our minds, partly because of the bare circumstances of the plot, but partly because the two speeches, that of the surrender, real or pretended, and the suicide farewell, are among the greatest things in Sophocles' plays. Both of them transform the pity into a perception of Ajax' dignity and majesty. The poetry of the first summons the universe into the fate of Ajax. Whether it is understood as a necessary deception of Tecmessa or as a genuine recantation, the extraordinary words present on the one side Ajax and on the other the universe in all its physical manifestations as matched antagonists. The passing of the seasons, the alternation of night and day, the interchange of sleep and waking, all assert the pattern of change as a condition of life. Only Ajax, till now, has stood for the immobility of timelessness. I quote:

> All things the long and numberless succession
> Of years brings into darkness; what was shown
> Is hidden. There is nothing we must not look for;
> The terrible oath, the strong hard spirit go down.
> I, once as stout and hard of heart as iron,
> Fresh from the dipping—my lips grow womanish,
> Brought to it by this woman. I pity her,
> Pity to leave her widowed among my enemies,
> Pity to leave my son an orphan. I
> Will go to the washing places, to the meadows
> And shun the heavy anger of the Goddess.
> And when I come there I will find a place,
> Untrodden, and will hide this sword of mine,
> This hated weapon, out of light, in earth.
> Let Night and Hades keep it down below.
> For from the day I had it from the hand
> Of Hector, gift of my bitterest enemy
> I have never had a good thing from the Greeks.
> It is the truth that men declare—an enemy's
> Gifts are no gifts; they bring no profit with them.
> So for the future I shall know to yield
> To gods and learn to reverence the Atreidae.
> They are my rulers, so I must yield to them.
> For things most dread and stouthearted give way
> To their authorities. This is the principle
> On which the snowy tracks of winter yield
> To the summer rich in harvest. This is why
> Night's dreary circle yields to the light of day's white team
> And thus the moaning sea has fallen asleep
> Under the breath of the dread winds. All-conquering sleep
> Fetters, but frees again and does not hold forever.
> Why should not I, then, learn discretion too?
> I know it only now: an enemy
> Should only be the object of our hate
> Insofar as he may one day be our friend;

And I would serve a friend only so far
As one that will not always so remain.
For most men friendship is a treacherous harbor.
Enough of this. Woman, go in and pray
The gods to gratify my heart's desire.
You, my friends, give me the same honor that she does.
Tell Teucer, if he comes, to care for me
And be your friend. For me
I must go where I must. Do as I say
And soon you may hear of me, although unlucky
Now, as of one that has won to his peace.

[ll. 645–92]

The killer is set where he will do his work
Most cuttingly—has one time to think of that?
A gift
Of Hector whom I hated most among
My foreign enemies, hated most to see.
And it is set in enemy earth, this Troyland,
New-whetted, with the iron-eating whetstone.
I have fixed it carefully, heedfully,
To be my best friend in the quickness of death.
That is all prepared, all good. Now next—
You first, O Zeus, who are rightly first, be gracious.
I shall ask you for a favor, not a great one.
Send me some messenger to Teucer bearing
This evil news, that he may be the first
To pick me up, as I fall here on the sword,
The blood still fresh upon it. Let me not
Be first spied by the enemy and thrown out
A prey to dogs and vultures.
Such is my supplication to you, O Zeus.
And with you I do call upon
The soul's guide, Hermes, Netherworld God,
To put me sound asleep—one quick short leap,
No struggling, the sword splitting my side apart.

I call on you to help, Eternal Virgins,
You that forever look upon all
That passes among men, you the long-shanked
Majestic Furies—mark me how I die
A victim of the Atreidae. Snatch them hence
By death as bad as they themselves are, ruin them,
As now you see me, taking my own life.
You quick avenging Furies, come come and taste;
Spare not the army, not the whole people.

Sun, you that drive your chariot in high heaven
When you look down upon my native land,
Check your rein, gold embroidered, give the news,
Of this my ruin and my death to my
Old father and my most unhappy mother.
Bitter indeed will be the cry she will raise
Through all the city as she learns my story.

But to the act and quickly. Death, death,
Come, be my overseer, now now,
And I shall soon address you, yours forever,
Upon the other shore.

You then, bright radiance,
That light this day, you Sun the Charioteer,
I call on you this last time and no more,
O light, O holy land of Salamis,
Hearth of my fathers, deep deep rooted,
Famed city of Athens and her breed of men,
Rivers and springs before me, plains of Troy,
I call
I call upon you all: goodbye to all.
You have all been my life. This then to you,
The last word Ajax speaks. And for the rest
I shall talk only with the dead below.

[ll. 815–65]

It is only when we have accepted entirely this, the dramatist's
conception of Ajax as a victim, but as a victim of a superhuman

magnificence, that the play allows us to catch a glimpse of another and more ordinary version of the story. We know that Athena is his enemy but we do not know, until the herald's speech, why she is his enemy. The herald tells us of Ajax' blasphemous words when his father gave him his blessing at leavetaking.

> "Son, be resolved always to win your fight
> but always win with God to help you win."
> Haughty and senseless was his answer:
> "Father, with gods to help, a nobody
> can win as well as any man. But I,
> even without them, trust to grasp renown."

[ll. 764–69]

It is quite clear that here we have the usual conventional comment on the cause of Ajax' downfall. The herald moreover quotes the prophet Calchas as linking the original boast to Athena's last chance to destroy him utterly, though her power to do so is mysteriously restricted to the following twenty-four hours, and by the condition that he must have left his tent and gone abroad. We are in fact given, on the surface at least, the reason for all the calamities in the play. What renders this reason insufficient is the effect of the dramatist's own workmanship. He has spent all his eloquence and power on making us sympathize with the hero and his side of the story.

No less striking in its paradoxical character is Sophocles' presentation of the attempted murder of the Atreidae, which was frustrated by Athena and turned into the disastrous attack on the cattle. Now it seems as if the projected assassination ought to merit dramatic emphasis. Agamemnon and Menelaus are the supreme commanders of the Greek army and as such are Ajax' commanders. Bowra indeed makes a great deal of Ajax' violation of his duty to his superior officers and certainly the sheer circumstances of the plot warrant what he has to say, if we can also find it in Sophocles.[6] The death of the Atreidae at the hands of another Greek must, one would think, be an appalling crime. Furthermore the attack is planned to be made on them at night when they were defenseless and asleep.

It could hardly be worse. In the actual execution not only are the cattle slaughtered and tortured but the unfortunate herdsmen were killed. And the reason? Ajax has a personal grudge against the princes because together with Odysseus, the successful candidate, they had deprived him of the arms of Achilles. For this they must all three die.

The sense of wounded personal honor in Ajax, and his violence in taking a personal revenge, is set in strong contrast with the position of Agamemnon and Menelaus. The princes are the spokesmen of the idea that the state is the unit of cohesion, in defense or attack. The man who cannot endure to be bound by its regulations puts himself out of ordinary civilized consideration. Ajax would be no man's subject—witness his personal refusal to accept the decision of the princes. So they wish to mark the sense of his outcast status by denying the corpse its burial rites.

If we agree that *Antigone* and this play were written within a couple of years of each other, it is likely that there was in Sophocles' mind, and perhaps in that of his contemporaries, a debate in progress over what inalienable rights, religiously or humanly guaranteed, a human creature could possess, when considered only as himself and not as a member of the body politic. In order to test the proposition at its most extreme Sophocles has presented two criminals, Polyneices and Ajax, as the most fundamentally outcast members of their societies, because of their voluntary acts. Polyneices had tried to destroy his city in civil war. Ajax had tried to kill his commanders in revenge for a personal insult. The case of both men is wrongly judged by the authorities in denying burial, which is due to the gods, be the corpse who he may.

But the play *Ajax* goes further. Odysseus ends his plea to

Agamemnon with the words: "It is not just to injure a good man once he is dead, however much you hate him" (ll. 1344–45). It is Ajax' claim to be a *good man,* in some sense, that is being tested by the decision to give or withhold burial. And the weight of the whole play to the moment of the suicide has been to make us enter sympathetically into the mental world of Ajax, where in stubborn suffering he faces as antagonists the gods and the community.

The attempted murder is a sin of violence as indisputably branded as a sin, as the offense of hybris is denounced by the herald. Neither of these things is conjured away by the dramatic treatment. But Sophocles is concerned with the metaphysical association of violence and stubbornness, antisocial in the Greek meaning of society, with some quality ultimately acceptable to the order of the universe, insofar as the latter is integrated with that of human society. The villain of today, promoted to saving potency, becomes his community's defender, once he has surrendered his humanity to death or destruction.

To tell this story it is important for the dramatist that the character of the sinner be deeply explored in his human pre-heroic condition. As this character is revealed from the inside, with this final vindication in mind, inevitably the weight of the counts against him are to some extent minimized, and the sense of the greatness of the personality overbears that of the crime. This is what happens in *Ajax.* We know of the attempted murder. It is a treacherous crime which in theory destroys the relation of man and society. But the society represented by Menelaus and his brother is petty and tyrannical. It has no use for a man of the size of Ajax. The shame inflicted on him by the superhuman powers overwhelms the sense of the offense of hybris. Ajax emerges as the image of one aspect of the human condition, eventually purged, as far as our interest goes, of the tangled facts of his guilt and his crime. That aspect of the human condition is an arbitrary subjection to the divine will, for both good and evil. He is also the image of a mystic connection between human evil—certain sorts of human evil, including hate, stubbornness, and arrogance—with the final potency of the hero in his transformed superhuman shape.

It is the subjection of humans to the divine will which also gives the play its unity. We are asked to look at a complicated situation stretching all the way from the scene when Ajax is exhibited, in his madness, for the benefit of his enemy Odysseus, to the struggle for the right to bury his brother waged by Teucer against the Atreidae. In this situation the heroes and villains are ostensibly shown in conventional terms, and then we are asked to regard them with Sophocles' special vision. The Sophoclean "eye" sees that "everything may happen when a god contrives" (l. 86). Therefore the conventional moral judgments are frequently wrong. They are wrong because they assume that the sinner is free to sin or not to sin and thus merits punishments or reproof. They are wrong because they assume that man reads the gods' judgment accurately and fully, and is therefore justified in implementing the sentence.

If we stop with the conventional judgment, Ajax is the man of violence and hybris who is punished by Athena for his offense, and for his attempted murder of the princes and Athena's favorite, Odysseus. He is driven to suicide by the power of Athena. Finally in the issue of the burial we see Odysseus as the arbitrator and wise counsellor, advising on the proper rights of god and human justice in the treatment of the dead.

But if we look closer and watch for the key lines—always so important in Sophocles—we can see a unity of feeling and theme which makes something different of the whole play. Odysseus is an important voice both at the beginning and the end. At the beginning he says, "I see that all mortal lives are shadows" (l. 126). "Everything may happen when a god contrives" (l. 86). And in the end he prevents Agamemnon from falling into the error of indulging his monarchical privilege of hating his dead enemy without regard to the enemy's mortality and his own. "You will not injure the dead man but the gods" (ll. 1343–44). If we see the play in this sense then, hybris acquires another significance. It is above all else, as every classical author tells us, thinking more than human thoughts. It is giving man's concepts and aspirations an absolute rather than a relative status. It is to believe that whatever I will as king or as warrior has an absolute value apart from whatever curious or mysterious role the gods have allotted me. Agamemnon and Menelaus are guilty of this offense and they come near to disaster, being saved only by Odysseus. Ajax *is* guilty of it on both counts, because he has challenged the goddess to a kind of duel and because in vindication of his personal honor he tries to murder the god-protected princes and Odysseus. As Ajax is guilty he pays the price in his lonely, agonizing death.

Hybris, the rebellion of man against the limitations of his human condition, takes various forms but is invariably punished. The subjection of man to the gods and the world they govern is the condition of human existence. Ambiguity arises when man justifies his own ethical standards by the outcome of, or rather by what he has decided to regard as the final outcome of, events in series. This may not be the final outcome. Hence human honor or disgrace in the community must either be taken as only human in their grounding or must be given provisional value as they depend on events which are controlled by the gods. Perhaps this can be expressed, without too much distortion, by a modern analogy.

Hybris may be conceived of as the action of a man stepping into a minefield. The location of the mines is not clearly charted but it is not quite unknown either. There are certain typical acts or words, like those of Ajax, or thoughts like those of Croesus in Herodotus, which are surely within the destructive power of the mines.

But there is a corollary. Some of those who are blown up by this method of ostensible self-destruction, so impersonally created and maintained by the gods, are chosen for a greater destiny later, once they have paid the mortal penalty. So no one knows or should think he knows what this minefield means exactly, in moral terms. Sensible men, in ordinary human relations, naturally do their utmost not to walk in any of the known locations of the mines. But they also know that this happens involuntarily, since the location at this point is not altogether known—and there are also men whom the gods seemingly lure into stepping into the area of destruction. Finally the strange destiny of those few who were destroyed and then raised to glory casts doubts in the minds of the wise on whether any safe moral inference can be drawn from the hybris and the divine punishment which immediately follows from it.

That this destiny is strange, rare, and miraculous, that it is indeed some extraordinary divine interference with the usual cosmic process, Sophocles thought. In *Ajax, Philoctetes,* and *Oedipus at Colonus* he presents a dramatic image of three of the stories where it happened, and the image is designed to make the man involved understood, while he was still man, and before he became a spirit and a hero.

It is hardly necessary to do as Whitman does—argue that the whole concept of hybris has become for Sophocles a meaningless conventional prejudice.[7] Nor perhaps are we on sufficiently firm ground with Abel, whose theory is that hybris when it is warranted by the stature of the hero-daemon is not hybris. According to Abel, it is only hybris when the sinner takes upon himself a privilege that after events prove was unjustified.[8] But we can surely put to ourselves the question: What does the dramatist intend our reaction to be to the herald's comments on Ajax' hybris or his attempt to murder the Atreidae? Has he so weighted them that we immediately see the balance between the crime and the punishment? Do we feel that the provocation of the god by Ajax' speech to his father is of the order of magnitude of the deception and suicide speeches? In other words, have we been given a cause *dramatically* satisfying for the destruction of Ajax? Perhaps we may be asked to see an ironic discrepancy between the pettiness of the god and the greatness of the hero. Or more probably Sophocles is suggesting a mistake in the human evaluation of the situation. Ajax is a chosen victim of the god because of, or in any case in conjunction with, his characteristic violence and intransigence. He is a *chosen* victim of the god and one day will be a chosen spirit that may protect the community with which he is associated. All that the ordinary man sees is the hybris, which provokes the god, and he regards it as causative in the vengeance upon Ajax. So it is, in a way. So it is from the standpoint of Athena, in her stage personality. Piety is the most important thing for mortals, she says. But this is perhaps only a partial expression of the divine will. The other part is the honored burial of the sinner's body and the heroic privileges of Ajax of Salamis and Athens. To think that Ajax' hybris, as expressed by the herald, is the antecedent cause of his downfall seems mistaken, as a dramatic explanation.

Finally there is the meaning of Ajax' death, and his relation to Athena. In several of the plays of Sophocles there are peculiar ambiguities which invest turns of character or even decisive movements of the plot. Who can be sure of all that is implied in Deianira's tampering with the magic of the shirt? Who can say with certainty why, in *Electra,* the Paedagogus is made to give such a strangely detailed and vivid account of the fictitious chariot race (ll. 680–763)? And here we must ask ourselves, probably also without finding one definite answer, what is the connection between Ajax' death and his feud with Athena? Is it, her last punishment of him, a sequel to the madness with which she afflicted him in the beginning of the play? Or is it to be understood as a voluntary act, a final moment of despairing defiance?

The Messenger's speech certainly points to the interpretation of Ajax' suicide as his final punishment by Athena. (It perhaps also lends strength to Bowra's notion that the goddess again drives him insane and that he kills himself when so possessed.)[9] He says that if Ajax can be kept within his tent for twenty-four hours, all will be well. "For only so long will the wrath of divine Athena harry him" (ll. 756–57). No explanation is given of why the anger of the goddess will be effective outside the tent and not inside. But since both the Messenger and the Chorus assume that Ajax' going out is the opportunity for Athena's anger, and they have the word of the prophet Calchas for it, and we next see Ajax in a lonely place by the shore, preparing to kill himself, it surely seems that his death is directly due to Athena's anger.

But this does not satisfy our sense of the dramatic weighting of the play. It leaves us committed to the most unlikely solution of the other main difficulty, the interpretation of the farewell speech at line 686. It would mean that we must accept this speech as Ajax' conversion to a more "ordinary" human ethic. He announces that he will submit to the Atreidae, though it is certainly not clear now, and still less from the speeches of Menelaus and Agamemnon later, what room there is for "submission" to the Atreidae, now that he has attempted to murder them. He justifies his conversion by referring to the analogy of the seasons and night and day, all of which, in their sequence, imply the surrender of one to the victorious other. He is disowning his position of uniqueness, and seeking to be like the rest of the world. He is now to be among the "tough and the strong" things that are eventually broken.

> I, once as stout and hard of heart as iron,
> Fresh from the dipping—my lips grow womanish,
> Brought to it by this woman [Tecmessa]. I pity her,
> Pity to leave her widowed among my enemies,
> Pity to leave my son an orphan.
>
> [ll. 648–53]

But the next time we see him, he is bent on suicide and there is no reference at all to the previous conversion. The death speech is as full of hatred of the Atreidae as were his earlier utterances and his sense of humiliation is overpowering enough to make him kill himself. There is no evidence in this speech for Bowra's contention that he is now insane again as he had been in the opening conversation with Athena.[10] Thus we have two speeches of blankly opposing content given to the same character within a short interval. Moreover both speeches are rich, for Sophocles peculiarly rich, in images and external analogies to make them emphatic in the meaning they bear for the whole play. There is only one key to their reconciliation given by the dramatist: Tecmessa herself believes that the first was intended solely to deceive her into abandoning her watchfulness as to Ajax' actions. Thus he escapes to the shore away from her on the pretext of offering sacrifice for his "new" life. And this explanation of the deception is indeed the only one that is acceptable if one takes into account the dramatist's own pointers. If this is right, Ajax' death is at once defiance of the goddess and his last payment to her, the voluntary acceptance by the hero of the last bitter dregs of his punishment.

This voluntariness must be properly understood. It is the anger of Athena which kills him but it does not kill an unsuspecting victim—as she had originally blunted his senses in the delusions of madness. This Ajax knows what he is doing. He goes to the death which Athena "causes" because he will not accept her world, the world of the pious (whom she exhorts Odysseus to emulate), of the cleverly temporizing Odysseus himself, of the power-conscious Atreidae, self-identified with the state, of the shifting alliances of friends and foes, yes, even the world whose symbolical succession of seasons and climate suggests impermanence and transition. Alone he has fought the cause of the unchanging and timeless against time, and now that he can fight it no more he will take his own life, a "victim" of Athena and her power. This, in a way, crystallizes his case against the world and the gods that rule it. It is natural that the poetry of this speech should be as rich and powerful as it is, for it is Ajax' farewell to all the associations that have so far constituted his life—his wife, his family, his soldiership. The depth of feeling here is, of course, entirely sincere, and is therefore given all the wealth of expression that it needs. All that is false is the inference which

Ajax pretends to draw—that because he now realizes the inevitability of the opposition between him and the "ordinary" world, he will submit to its rules and its practices. When we understand that this speech is really one of rejection of the alternative of a life of submission, we see shadows of the emergence of a new spirit, neither exactly man nor god—the hero Ajax of Salamis.

Yet we are left with several unsolved riddles. What are we to make of the undying opposition of Athena, this member of the Olympian hierarchy, to the hero-spirit to be, and why is her power over him so curiously circumscribed in time and space? No explanation of questions like these is much more than a guess. But perhaps what is implied is that the divine world is not single in its view of Ajax; that Athena's resentment of his hybris and his murder attempt is in some respects at variance with the divine purposes for Ajax which are to lead to his elevation to the status of hero. Perhaps Sophocles is following the lead of Homer and Herodotus where a particular god may, either for good or ill, control the destiny of a man, but only until the moment that his fate is final and irrevocable. Then the lesser divine intervention ceases. But if this is the way to take it, it still appears likely that Sophocles is giving a traditional and allegorical version on the surface of what in fact is a new religious meaning for the story. What he means is that Ajax is of the order of the new and original elements of the human world which are indispensable in the relation of god and man in communities.

At line 835 the suicide speech of Ajax contains a remarkable passage:

> I call on you to help, Eternal Virgins,
> You that forever look on all
> That passes among men, you the long-shanked
> Majestic Furies—mark me how I die
> A victim of the Atreidae. Snatch them hence
> By death as bad as they themselves are, ruin them,
> As now you see me, taking my own life.

What is the meaning of "a victim of the Atreidae"? (Literally: see how I, wretched, am destroyed by the Atreidae.) It must refer either to the original decision to award Achilles' arms to Odysseus rather than Ajax or to the imminent threat of execution and torture which the vengeance of the princes now suspends over him. In either case the logic is peculiar. For the act which precipitated Ajax' madness and subsequent humiliation was his own plan to murder the Atreidae. This was *his* vengeance for their wrong to him and from it, for the second time, starts Athena's resentment. And equally it is because of the murder attempt that he is now compelled to choose death at his own hand rather than theirs. What he is doing in the speech is to arraign the Atreidae and their backers, divine and human, for being the *occasion* of his fall, and he so arraigns them before some divine tribunal greater and more august, and therefore more susceptible of understanding his unique value. These powers will come to *his* aid in time—at least, will punish those who have conspired to destroy him. Ajax has parted company with the ethics of the ordinary fifth-century man—which of course is the anachronistic moral climate in which fifth-century tragedy lives—and considers himself a being apart whose rights are unchallengeable and whose anger once provoked must find scope. He is on the way to consider himself a demigod and a demigod humiliated.

There is something reminiscent of the Prometheus story in this one. In the Aeschylus play Prometheus also appeals for "justice" (l. 1092), though in helping man in defiance of the decree of Zeus he has forfeited any claim to the ordinary "justice" in the divine order. It is hard to say how important it is that both Prometheus and Ajax appeal to the elements of the physical world—the sun and sky—and that both feel that the Furies, perhaps truly as representatives of the old gods, are on their side in the end.[11] That Ajax also appeals to Zeus probably only means that he turns from the lesser and more definable divinity of his persecutor Athena to the more vaguely apprehended supreme power of the Olympians. This is, of course, not possible inside of the context of the Aeschylean play.

I do not imply that there is any conscious echo of *Prometheus* in *Ajax*. But it does suggest that perhaps Sophocles, too, is reaching out to a dramatization of some similar cosmic force in its inception and formation. Prometheus changed the lot of man by his defiance of the gods. In the end, having suffered torture, and in virtue of his knowledge of the threat that hangs over Zeus, he finds his way to a new and stable relation to Zeus and the world of the gods—and man has attained a new dimension quite different from his primitive animal condition. I am suggesting that Ajax is the first representative of Sophocles' three maimed heroes, victims and latent potencies, who, through their sufferings and inner powers, will finally protect their communities against their enemies, themselves in a hierarchical position between gods and men. Sophocles is showing us Ajax in the last stage of his suffering in the progress between man and spirit. At this moment the ranks of the gods above him—here, Athena—can still persecute him. But only for a time. The way lies through his death to his final power, which he attains with some form of Divine approbation, foreshadowed by his winning of burial at the end of this play. Had he stayed in his tent, had he not gone to meet his death by the seashore and the last punishment by Athena, he would not have been Ajax. In this sense Athena the persecutor is also the agent of his final elevation to honor. But to see it this way is, I am sure, a mistake. It is much more probable that Sophocles and his contemporaries thought of divine powers that did in fact face both ways. Athena is the punisher, the avenger whose anger against Ajax may be indulged to the infliction of the utmost punishment, in this case death. But this death in the Sophoclean play is also a last payment. Ajax says to his wife and followers, as he takes leave of them: "Do as I say and soon you may hear of me, although unlucky now, as of one that has won to his peace" (ll. 691–92). For him the words surely mean only "out of the reach of persecution of man and god." But in the context of the whole play they have a wider significance. He has won to the position of hero-spirit and it is his vindication in this capacity that is implied in the granting of burial and the acknowledgments of Odysseus.

This play is concerned with the *events* of Ajax' destruction. It *implies* a meaning concerning the conjunction of the destruction and final honor of this unique man. The character of Ajax is barely and starkly rendered. The personality is not presented in much detail nor is the situation treated in detail. Both these aspects of the dramatic theme are expanded in the two later plays, *Philoctetes* and *Oedipus at Colonus*.

Philoctetes

Philoctetes was apparently produced about 409 B.C., when Sophocles was eighty. Among the other plays of Sophocles it has always seemed peculiar because of its unique technical features, notably the deus ex machina (Heracles' ghost) and the "happy" ending.[12] Nowhere else does Sophocles use the deus ex machina, which is so common in Euripides. And nowhere else does Sophocles present tragedy with a conclusion which does not involve suffering and death as the logical outcome of the preceding actions—unless *Oedipus at Colonus* can be so seen. It may be, of course, that had we more tragedies of Sophocles we would find that both he and Euripides were making much the same experiments in workmanship, as both tried innovations in the formalized construction of Greek tragedy at about the same time—the last twenty years of their competitive theatrical careers. Many critics indeed have written of *Philoctetes* as something akin to the lighter half-tragic, half-sentimental work of Euripides, like *Helen*.

But whether in fact *Philoctetes* was historically as unique as it appears to us, the important thing is to understand what effects Sophocles was seeking when he employed the "happy ending"—which in general Aristotle censures as inappropriate to tragedy. What is there about *Philoctetes* that leads Sophocles to dispense with his usual conclusion of death and destruction? And if we ask that question we are inclined to make a discovery: that for some reason the plot of *Philoctetes* as an image of life— and this really means as a story in the simplest sense—comes much closer to modern feeling than nearly any other Greek tragedy. Has this something to do with the ending, in spite of what seems to us the very undramatic quality of the deus ex machina?[13]

Now perhaps it is true that we are more susceptible in our histrionic emotions to images of death's equivalent—mental breakdown, collapse of a personality, end of a relationship—than that of physical destruction itself. Perhaps the latter has become too crude a stage symbol for us; it may be that our fear of death has grown less and our fear of transformation or degeneration more. But whatever the reason, one of the really exciting things for a modern reader of *Philoctetes* is that the end has for him something attractive *because* it is thoroughly enigmatic and ironical. It suggests questions in a very modern vein. Why does *Philoctetes* not yield before he does? Or more properly: Why does he yield only to Heracles' arguments, having held out both against his enemy Odysseus and his friend Neoptolemos? What is he giving up when he returns to Troy? And (most puzzling of all and a question to ask ourselves although it also involves Sophocles) why is it that a piece of us, anyway, does not *want* him to yield, for his own good, and go to Troy? Had the end of the play been the death of the hero on his island resisting to the last the efforts of friend and enemy to ship him to Troy, we would have had an unequivocal symbol of the dramatist's meaning. Philoctetes would have met his tragic and appropriate fate. Noble or mistaken, his gesture would have been unambiguously accommodated to our notions of him. Sometimes we can rise to the simple grandeur of such a conclusion as the representation of final victory or defeat. But more often we prefer as a superior truth some representation of the doubtfulness of the values for which the hero made his sacrifice, although he still makes it, or some sign of his "ordinary" weaknesses among his extraordinary qualities. In something of this way *Philoctetes* leaves us in a very mixed mood at the end. We do not quite know exactly what the dramatist *means* by the end. Is Philoctetes' return to Troy a good thing, or only an inevitable thing? Why, if it is the first, does the final action fall so flatly and unhappily? If it is only inevitable, what aspect of reality as the destroyer of the tragic vision is being here caught by the poet?

This is the second version of Sophocles' maimed hero. It is far more explicit than that of Ajax because he is far more human and we know far more about him. We can observe the various shades of acceptance or rejection of him by his fellow men. We are going to look at his dilemma through several different eyes instead of seeing it only through his. We are going to see not only how *he* feels but how his feelings make a difference to the outcome insofar as they affect the other actors.

For the effect of *Philoctetes* rests on the possibility that the end may be different. Philoctetes may return to Troy or he may not. He may persuade Neoptolemos to take him home or he may not. It is even possible to conclude (with some reserves about the oracle) that his captors may take him to Troy unwillingly or not. Ajax had really no such alternatives. His death is the only possible solution. The purpose of *Ajax* is to give the audience a passionate sense of the suffering of the main actor. The proper conclusion to that feeling is the shock and awe awakened by his death. But in the later play we are asked as much to understand as to pity. We are led delicately to learn what our sympathies for

Philoctetes imply for social or political life. Some end there must be which suggests the summation of this strange profit-and-loss account between Philoctetes and the Greeks, but it cannot be an unequivocal emotional symbol like death.

At first we have what seems to be a simple sort of plot and a simple appeal to our feelings. Somewhat deceptively, the play appears to turn more around Neoptolemos than Philoctetes.[14] Neoptolemos is used as a tool by Odysseus for carrying out his intention of capturing Philoctetes. From the beginning we are aware of some hesitation on the part of the young man and so are partly prepared for his change of mind later. Everything is done to make us feel that Philoctetes is a victim. He is alone, suffering, ragged, and crippled. He is pitiably anxious for the smallest token of community with his fellow beings; even the interchange of words is something to be treasured (ll. 228–31, 234–35). Neoptolemos gradually comes to feel that plans for his own glory cannot be carried through at the expense of this wretched relict of the older line of the Greek heroes of the Trojan War. So he gives back the bow, the one tangible advantage he has gained from Odysseus' stratagems, formally disassociates himself from Odysseus and tries to persuade Philoctetes, in a frank and open way, to join him in the enterprise against Troy. His arguments fail to convince, but the opportune appearance of the ghost of Heracles, Philoctetes' old comrade and the donor of the bow, achieves what Neoptolemus has not been able to do, and Philoctetes leaves the island to find healing at Troy and renown in arms again, by the side of his young rescuer.

Seen this way, the play is concerned with the dilemma of Neoptolemos, who is forced to choose between humanity and political considerations. As he comes to understand more fully what each of the two positions means, in regard to Philoctetes, he chooses the former and is rewarded by eventually winning the political advantages, without paying the price of the sacrifice of his honor which Odysseus' scheme would have involved. There is some truth in seeing the play like this, but it is only the truth which lies on the surface. The other aspects of the plot which the dramatist exposes are much profounder, but also much more ambiguous.

The first evidence of ambiguity in the presentation is the nature of Philoctetes' final surrender. For it is not to the arguments of Neoptolemos that he yields but to the orders of Heracles' ghost. If the play really deals with Neoptolemos' moral enlightenment, or even, stretching a point, with the moral conflict of Odysseus and Philoctetes in which the young man chooses the weaker and better side, Philoctetes should certainly be graciously influenced to oblige Neoptolemos, who is prepared to give up so much for him. He does nothing of the sort. He is as obdurate to Neoptolemos' last plea, though now without anger, as he had been to Odysseus' threats. If it be said that Philoctetes is *gradually* succumbing to persuasion and that the appearance of Heracles is only the last straw, it is still apparent that it is the ghost's appearance that *is* the last straw and it seemingly adds something important to the case. This must lie in the relation of Heracles to Philoctetes, for, as far as his arguments go, they have all been used on Philoctetes before. Personally I go much further. I believe that the appearance of Heracles makes a radical transformation in Philoctetes' position, that in fact he dare not disobey the demigod who overrules all the objections which till then retained their validity in Philoctetes' mind. Thus we are made to speculate on the reasons for Philoctetes' final refusal of Neoptolemos, and this shifts our interest from what Neoptolemos is inspired to do, and whether he succeeds, to what the projected action meant for Philoctetes as a person.

The second ambiguity shows itself in our own hesitation how to accept Philoctetes' refusal of Neoptolemos' offer. We have so far certainly been on his side. But when, unconstrained and undeceived, he refuses Neoptolemos for the last time, we are conscious of uneasiness. Not an uneasiness such that we can speak like the Chorus, who censures Philoctetes as an obstinate fool. But uneasy because we are no longer sure that he is right, morally, as he was in his fight against Odysseus—and yet we do not exactly want him to go with Neoptolemos either.

With these ideas in mind let us reconsider the play. It is a story about a hero whose rejection by society lies far in the past and whose restoration is so necessary and so ordained by the gods that there is no room for the interplay of former friendships or enmities over its desirability. Thus the feeling and sentiment involved in the original expulsion exist solely in the victim. For other people, friends and foes, he exists only insofar as he is a new and important factor in the winning of victory. We are made to see through his eyes what sort of sacrifice is demanded of him. We are also made to look at his actions from the point of view of a complete stranger and an entirely uncomprehending former enemy. What began as the account of a plot where there is a split between the conspirators ends by focusing on the victim. The plot is still of central importance, since we care most about the turn of events—will Philoctetes be shipped off either by deception or force, and what will become of him afterwards? But the play is really concerned with the implications expressed by the words and deeds of the three protagonists. It is truer of this Greek play than of most others that the characters are closely articulated because in the greater detail lies much of the meaning of the issues.

Neoptolemos' chief qualities are inexperience, ambition, and a certain natural generosity—in that order. The dialogue between him and Odysseus, with which the play opens, shows that Odysseus was wise to select this boy as his accomplice. Not only because Neoptolemos' youth saves him from the suspicions of Philoctetes which attach to members of the Trojan expedition and which would align him either with the foes or with the friends of Philoctetes' past, but because only through someone as innocent as Neoptolemos could Odysseus work. Neoptolemos is no personal friend of Odysseus but he is the next best thing. He is awed by his selection to a "joint" command with one of the older great heroes of the Trojan War. His deep feeling for his father's greatness is backed by no personal knowledge of him (ll. 350–51). What he is set to emulate is the greatness of an unknown. Neoptolemos is so suitable as a tool for Odysseus because he has no notion of the opposition which exists between the kind of man he wants to be and Odysseus' orders. He is somewhat uncomfortable about the plan for Philoctetes' capture. It does appear as through a number of armed men ought to be able to deal with a single cripple even armed with a bow, without resorting to treachery and lies. But Odysseus plays on Neoptolemos' vulnerable side very skillfully. He is under orders to assist, not criticize. It is an order emanating not from Odysseus himself but from the general council of the Greeks. Odysseus himself once felt exactly as Neoptolemos does but now he knows better: "The tongue is mightier than the sword." Besides, in this case, the magic bow is indeed something more than the ordinary sword, and Neoptolemos himself on reflection doubts the wisdom of a straightforward effort at capture. Neoptolemos in his youthful simplicity never grasps what will be the real difficulty—how to persuade Philoctetes to cooperate, either on the island or thereafter when he is on the ship. Odysseus knows all about this. As the event proves he anticipates the attempts at suicide and has thought of psychological means to counteract them—the threat to use the bow without its owner, so that Philoctetes will see that his suicide will be quite ineffective as revenge on his enemies.

Neoptolemos is also ambitious and has not yet realized the implications of Odysseus' kind of ambition. That ambition is simply the will to win by any means. Odysseus is explicit in asserting that there is no single code to which he adheres except the will to win; that there is no conjunction of a kind of action and his own disposition such that one can say, "He will do this, and never that." On the contrary:

> As the occasion
> Demands, such a one am I.
> When there is a competition of men just and good,
> You will find none more scrupulous than myself.
> What I seek in everything is to win. . . .
>
> [ll. 1048–52]

Philoctetes and Odysseus illustrate two different values of "nature" and the boy shows the wavering of the young mind between the two before coming down on the side of Philoctetes. What Odysseus stands for is a universal flexibility at the service of one's aims. Words have a unique value for him because they are the currency which is valid in the world, a standard value for a standard coin. Most men not only believe in the identity of a man's nature and certain acts, but they also believe in the meaning of words attached to these acts—good, base, honorable, dishonorable. Not so Odysseus, for whom words have no special meaning apart from their usefulness in their given setting.

> For one brief shameless portion of a day
> Give me yourself, and then for all the rest
> You may be called most scrupulous of men.
>
> [ll. 83–85]

> You shall be called a wise man and a good.
>
> [l. 119]

Thus for Odysseus there is always an opposition between the substance and the meaning of an act—which is related solely toward attainment of an ultimate objective—and the official title which the act possesses.

To some extent Odysseus in this play is not represented simply as a cunning manipulator. Rather he is the experienced man who tells the boy the way the world *is*. The initial dialogue is there to set in perspective the issues inherent in the play's action. Odysseus is the believer in the practical value of morality which declares that there is no real tendency in a sensible man to identify himself with any code of ethics except the struggle for aggrandizement. The highest form of aggrandizement is power, and power consists in using other people. In the mind of the fifth-century version of Odysseus, power is most effectively won and used as the servant, at best the high servant, of the state. Hence the emphasis in Odysseus' speeches on the importance of delegation of authority. "Nature" in man means simply this will to power, and the wish to avoid pain and damage. There is therefore also no special value in courage—Odysseus flies before Philoctetes when he has the bow in his hands.

Philoctetes stands for the idea that human nature, even in extremity and perversity, has a grasp on essentials in the world which are guaranteed by some divine power. Man's concepts of honor and dishonor ought to be and, although at times Philoctetes *almost* despairs, *are,* he thinks, in harmony with the order of the gods. But the seeming indifference of these "gods" to his own case, and the implications of all Neoptolemos' account of his former friends and foes at Troy—the success of the villains and the death and misery of the just—shake Philoctetes' belief in the identity of his concept of "justice" and the order of the Olympians. However, he sticks stubbornly to his belief that the nature of man is set in accordance with objective rules of morality. Violation of these results in self-destruction. He sticks to his own sense of having been wronged. He sees what he has suffered as an injustice and therefore, whatever the gods that guarantee it, he sees it as wicked and not to be belittled.

For years Philoctetes has been reduced to the satisfaction of the simplest natural needs—the most elementary kind of food, heat, shelter, and the reduction of his pain. He has been without society, without the use of language, without anything except thought to distinguish him from the animals. In his address to his island and the beasts he preyed on we can see the dynamic power that this life had exerted over his imagination. For his thoughts, he lived on the implications of a single act performed ten years ago. The anger generated by this wrong has kept him in life, and his heroism (to himself) consists in surviving, and surviving more or less sane ("I think the sight itself would have been enough to break down anyone except myself" [ll. 535–37]). So his story had become a kind of archetypal experience. Neoptolemos at once gains his confidence because he tells a story something similar. In a world where injustice, ingratitude, and knavery are the ways of success Philoctetes has no more to do than Ajax.

The boy finally stands by this concept of nature rather than that of Odysseus. It is what in the end puts him on Philoctetes' side. But he is, of course, committed to the superior practical value of returning to Troy. He has nothing to turn the other scale. He does not know personally the quality of wrong and hatred which belongs to Philoctetes. He will learn later. Here he is the young thing who is "naturally" good—which in social terms, for Sophocles, means treating others like yourself rather then as counters. He sacrifices many advantages to align himself so.

But it is surely remarkable how very sharply Sophocles has chosen to mark the limits of Neoptolemos' decency. It is clear that he is prepared to go a very long way in applying pressure to Philoctetes. He leaves him alone, except for the watchful presence of the Chorus at line 1070, while he and Odysseus ostensibly make ready to sail. Whether we assume that this move of Odysseus is a supreme bluff to break Philoctetes' resistance or the expression of a deliberate intention to abandon him on the island to starve, Neoptolemos goes along with it. He takes a very long time to come to himself, to realize that he cannot win his objective at such a price of torturing another human being. Furthermore, having given back the bow to Philoctetes, he makes a most determined attempt to persuade Philoctetes into doing what Odysseus would have tricked him into doing. One cannot resist the impression that Neoptolemos in returning the bow to Philoctetes may have been motivated not only by concern for his own self-respect, but somewhat by the idea that he has a better chance of persuading

Philoctetes on his own, and with clean hands. It is true that when Philoctetes again refuses he honorably accepts the refusal, and that his fears for reprisals against himself and his country are stilled by Philoctetes' offers of help; but, all in all, we can see with absolute certainty that Neoptolemos is no nearer understanding Philoctetes at the end than at the beginning. That Philoctetes should decline healing and the chance of glory is stupid and wrongheaded and most inconvenient for Neoptolemos. There is something important in Sophocles' presentation of the necessary conjunction of persons and powers for the final defeat of Troy—the young and the old with the same philosophical principles, but the one with the clearheadedness bred of want of experience and suffering, the other with the fears and passions of the past to blur his decisions and to sharpen his sense of what is involved in them. And both are united for this task of destiny, the reduction of Troy, by the possession of the magic bow. Heracles had passed it on to Philoctetes, a reward for his help. Philoctetes explicitly recalls this when, at a similar moment of gratitude, he allows Neoptolemos to handle it and leaves it in his possession when he faints with pain. In some way the bow's ownership marks Philoctetes as unique, as Heracles had been before him. Heracles speaks of the bow as the transmitted gift that shall again destroy Troy. He also speaks of the destined association of Philoctetes, the bow, and the young Neoptolemos.

Yet indeed the play, at least in several of its stages, leaves us in doubt about the destiny of Philoctetes and his bow—must they be together or can they be separated—and the question that is thereby involved: How much voluntary cooperation must be got from Philoctetes in order to have the desired results? We must take it that the oracle which is so often quoted in the play, and so diversely, is the proper authority for the gods' intentions.

We first hear of the oracle from Odysseus—though he merely states the position as a fact without specifically attributing it to the words of Helenus the prophet. This comes later. He says to

Neoptolemos: "If this man's bow shall not be taken by us, you cannot sack the town of Troy" (ll. 68–69). From the beginning, notice, the oracle links Philoctetes' bow and Neoptolemos' presence. It is probable that the hint we get here is later amplified into the notion of a succession of Neoptolemos to Philoctetes as Philoctetes succeeded Heracles as the bow's possessor. But if the oracle is clear about the conjunction of Neoptolemos and the bow ("not you apart from it nor it from you" [l. 115]) it is certainly not so clear about whether the bow must be wielded by its present owner, Philoctetes. In fact it is probably true to say that the play never makes us absolutely certain that Philoctetes' physical presence at Troy is necessary, if the conspirators can secure the bow. Originally, Odysseus tells the young man that he should "ensnare the soul of Philoctetes with your words" (ll. 54–55). Persuasion will not work and neither will force, which are the alternatives Neoptolemos would prefer. Presumably what this means—in the light of Odysseus' instructions—is that Neoptolemos should tell a story convincing enough to get Philoctetes aboard complete with bow. It gives us no sure indication what Odysseus' course will be after that, whether he trusts to Philoctetes' recognition of the necessity of cooperating with him, once he is a prisoner, or whether he will really be able to use the bow himself or get Teucer to do so as he later says. We cannot tell from this part of the play whether Philoctetes himself has been given by the oracle an undisputed role in Troy's capture. The bow certainly has.

We get another account of the oracle from Odysseus' sailor, disguised as a trader. Helenus prophesied that they would never capture Troy "till they persuaded Philoctetes to come with them and leave this island" (ll. 612–13). This would certainly seem to settle the matter, were it not that the disguised trader is only an agent of Odysseus, and therefore may be expected to say just what is useful for the moment. All this establishes, then, is that Odysseus wants instilled in Philoctetes' mind the idea that Odysseus is in pursuit of him, with a mandate from the state, and that he must "persuade" Philoctetes to accompany him. It is possible that this true reporting of the oracle, if it is such, is only intended to scare and infuriate Philoctetes till he will readily embark with Neoptolemos, should he happen to have any doubts about the bona fides of his new friend. But if the oracle had not spoken of the cooperation of Philoctetes, it is hard to imagine why Odysseus should have mentioned the detail of the "persuasion," since at this moment it hardly helps the case in Philoctetes' mind. He is much too angry at the idea that Odysseus should assume that he could be persuaded.

Neoptolemos, in his private conversation with the Chorus, says straight out that the bow without Philoctetes is worthless. *This* should be definitive, except that Odysseus implies the exact opposite, a little later, when he threatens Philoctetes with abandonment on the island while the Greeks use his bow. We are not quite sure whether this is bluffing, or quite sure whether Odysseus and Neoptolemos are bluffing when they go to the boat, ostensibly with the intention of sailing away. If Philoctetes comes to a better frame of mind, good; if not, they will take the sailors (the Chorus) and go without him. Perhaps this is intended to give the final turn of the screw to Philoctetes' resolution, as he finds himself within minutes of being forsaken and slowly starving on his island. But, if so, there is no clear recognition that this is so. We are certainly made to feel that Philoctetes is daring the ultimate in refusing to go with them. These obscurities and ambiguities are inherent in the Greek view of fate and in the way in which the dramatist used that view in his theater.

What the fifth-century theatergoer meant by fate was a shadowy road, with numerous turns and bypaths, the road's destination being hinted at, threateningly or encouragingly, by authorities of no very certain credibility. In the story of Philoctetes, the bow is essential, the bow's owner probably essential, though not certainly. If Philoctetes refuses stubbornly enough, the other side in the contest will try to do without him. Perhaps in that case the gods will refuse victory, but Odysseus and his friends are not sure enough of this to abandon an effort to take a short cut to the prophecy's conclusion.

This is clearly a very convenient kind of theology against which to set a play, for the playwright has, ready-made, the audience's acceptance of doom, and at the same time the efforts of the characters to alter the line of destiny are not looked upon as impious or irrational. What everyone in the play tries to do is to act as he would without anything in mind that could be called fatalism. What is startling—and of course tragic, in the theatrical sense—is that on looking backwards we see the original prediction to be true and, in the rearward mirror, to have had a compelling truth. But the road is, of course, very different from what we imagined it would be. The oracle or the prophecy marks the point of dramatic attention. This is where we are going. It colors with somber certainty all the actions that follow. But the persons on the stage must act, even if their hearts are full of fear of the fulfillment of the prophecy. They can only act with their reason as a guide to what is proper to be done. In this play we do not know whether the oracle was represented as specifying Philoctetes *and* the bow, along with Neoptolemos, or only the bow and Neoptolemos. Perhaps the oracle had only mentioned the bow and Neoptolemos and in view of the great difficulty in handling it—the bow from Homer on, right down to the fifth century, was looked on as a strange and exotic weapon, and this was Heracles' magic bow—Odysseus and others jumped to the conclusion that this necessarily implied bringing its owner. Later, in the face of his determined resistance, and infuriated by what appears to be his irrationality, Odysseus decides to try what can be done with the bow without Philoctetes, and Neoptolemos is fairly sure that he is going to go through with the attempt.

There are three points of climax in the plot and all are subject to difficulties of interpretation. The first is the return of the bow to Philoctetes by Neoptolemos; the second is the refusal of Philoctetes to go to Troy, even with the bow back in his own hands; the third is the "persuasion" of Philoctetes by the ghost of Heracles.

Neoptolemos' decision to give back the bow to Philoctetes marks one formal victory for Philoctetes. For the plot is concerned with the struggle between Odysseus and Philoctetes for the mind of the young Neoptolemos. Odysseus starts with all the advantages. Neoptolemos looks up to him as a man older, more experienced, and, inferentially anyhow, wiser. Furthermore Odysseus is Neoptolemos' commander and stands as an expert in state business to this tyro. Against this, Philoctetes has nothing to set except his wretchedness and his courage. To exploit these further, while refraining from any sympathetic identification with them, which is what Odysseus asks Neoptolemos to do, finally contradicts the boy's personal sense of honor and integrity. Giving back the bow is an exceedingly generous act, for it means the sacrifice of the glory assured him by the oracle and offered him by the Greek leaders. It means also that Neoptolemos has chosen to regard his inner knowledge of himself as a man of honor as a superior reality to the most objective marks of honor by others. It means that Odysseus has lost the battle of meaning, where he had claimed that good and bad winning is all the same, as long as it is winning, that words are only conscious expressions of momentary feelings or pretended feelings, and that the final achievement of objectives is the only sensible measuring stick.

In a study of Sophocles' political meaning, the conversion of Neoptolemos is also crucial. He is saying that the young and unspoiled will incline toward decency, which means treating others like yourself. It means that they implicitly accept the idea that the world is controlled by unpredictable gods and that misfortune is often unmerited. They do not see the world as a game of manipulative catch-as-catch-can, with the prizes of success as the only things worth having—as Odysseus does.

But the young Neoptolemos also does not understand the dilemma of Philoctetes, and it is this dilemma, marked by Philoctetes' final refusal of Neoptolemos' renewed request that he come to Troy, that probes the deepest meaning of the play.

Philoctetes is now in no sense under constraint. He has his bow in his hands. He is no worse off, as far as his island life is concerned, than before Neoptolemos landed—except for the resurrection of the hope of home-coming. Even in this Philoctetes is winning. For reluctant as Neoptolemos is to give up Troy and his chance of distinction, he will give it all up and bring Philoctetes home to Oeta. So Philoctetes' refusal of Neoptolemos is an entirely voluntary decision, as nothing else has been, exactly, since we first saw him on the stage. Neoptolemos now pushes sensibly and relentlessly all the reasonable arguments. "You are sick and the pain of sickness is of god's sending. . . . You will never know relief . . . until you come . . . to Troy." The gods have promised that "all Troy must fall this summer. . . . Trust the gods, my word, and, with me as friend, fare forth" (ll. 1326, 1338–41, 1373–75); and, especially the note of implied condemnation:

> The fortunes that the gods give to us men
> We must bear under necessity.
> But men that cling willfully to their sufferings
> As you do, no one may forgive nor pity.
>
> [ll. 1316–20]

Philoctetes is trying to fight off his special destiny and remain a man. The man has been desperately injured. He is being asked to give up the sense of injury which alone has enabled him to live all these years on the island. It is because of his response to his wrong that he is an individual. Odysseus has failed to reduce him, by bribes or violence, to a cipher in the state's contest of victory or defeat. That the boy has deserted Odysseus for himself is proof that his own kind of man is still left in the world, that they are not quite vanished with the old comrades of Troy now dead and gone, that his and their values are not false.

But yet in the order of the universe Philoctetes is not to be allowed to indulge his humanity. He is not the instrument of Odysseus for the Greeks' purposes, but he is also not a free agent. He is the servant of destiny, a magical force that must be harnessed for some purpose that pointedly ignores human feelings. For Neoptolemos the inducements of healing and glory would be decisive. He has never known Philoctetes' anger and pain. His humanity is not deep enough yet, because he is not old enough. Even in his estimate of the total situation he is hopelessly simpleminded. The odds against Philoctetes' escape from future treachery at the hands of the Atreidae are overwhelming. "It is not the sting of wrongs past, but what I must look for in wrongs to come," says Philoctetes (ll. 1358–59). If he is a man with ordinary human feelings, he is moving straight to the near certainty of being injured just as he was before. Worse, as he will be working for Odysseus and the Atreidae, the very men who ruined him—however much this is camouflaged by the association with Neoptolemos—he will have denied the *lasting* meaning of that act of theirs, and the meaning which he had created out of his survival in defiance of their attempt to destroy him. For the last time, in defense of his own humanity and individuality, in defense of his curiously personal creation, his life on the island, he refuses everything that Neoptolemos now offers.

How, as an audience, we take this depends on our interpretation of the appearance of Heracles. We know that, in a way, we wish Philoctetes to persist in his rejection of what is still the plan of the Atreidae for him. But the play is so weighted that we are prepared for something to break him down. Indeed at some level of receptiveness we *want* something to break him down. But there is in us, too, a feeling for something which transcends in man his ordinary humanity—the heroic. The heroic is not only being greater than other men in the qualities they possess. It is possessing certain qualities they do not have at all.[15]

The bow is the symbol of Philoctetes' uniqueness, and his uniqueness among men carries with it the necessity of being the bow's servant as well as its master. It has been his power to survive. Without it, when Odysseus had stolen it, he sees nothing for himself on the island but a lingering death. It is the transmitted gift of Heracles, at his moment of leaving the human world, and it is in some sense shared by Philoctetes with Neoptolemos, who is to be his associate and perhaps his successor. The power of the bow is what gives him a power quite different from that of other men. Heracles speaks to him as the former owner of the bow, his predecessor too in the checkered fortunes, the overriding of personal feelings, which go with its possession.

The bow is the gift of those enigmatic gods who rule the world. If you are the unique being to whom it is entrusted they do not indulge you in the ordinary privilege of other humans—to love your friends and hate your enemies. You are not permitted to give a special value to your experience of the past as an index of the future, nor to the integrity of your loves or hates. The divine order which, earlier in the play, as Philoctetes listens to Neoptolemos telling of the fortunes of war, is so clearly on the side of the rascals is also, with uncomfortable versatility, on the side of the just men as well. So when your time comes, you must accept it.

You cannot, as man, abandon your hatred and the pain which caused it, for these, in fact, are proofs of the reality of the single act. (In *Oedipus at Colonus* Creon links anger and pain and says of the latter, "it is only the dead that pain does not touch" [l. 955].) But the sense of pain, and hatred, must be shelved. For you must master your personal humanity to serve your unique function as a power, for protection of the political community, and for the destruction of its enemies.

This is not, of course, Odysseus' concept of the relation of the individual—this peculiar individual—to the state but it has a paradoxical similarity to it. For both Odysseus and Philoctetes must treat personal feelings as irrelevant. They must fight solely to win. They must be the servants of the destiny which the gods dictate to the state. But the difference is that in Odysseus there is no humanity to struggle against. He is incapable of ultimate hatred, as we see at the end of *Ajax*. Unlike Ajax himself, Odysseus hates only as long as there is any proper exercise for the hatred. He is also incapable of love or friendship, as this play would indicate.[16]

The play's point of emphasis is the struggle within Philoctetes between the sense of his own humanity and the necessity of obeying the impersonal task imposed on him by the gods. The stroke of these gods separated him from his community. He has been wronged, insulted, mortally injured by those of his community who have assumed that the god's branding of him is reason sufficient for discarding the victim from their midst, on sheer grounds of self-interest. The tragedy covers the last moments of the hero-spirit's humanity when, still with full consciousness of what he has suffered, he recognizes enemies turned friends; recognizes that they view his present usefulness as mechanically as they had his former offensive disadvantages. He must almost simultaneously become aware of himself as a man and something near to a god, and must sacrifice the man to the spirit. The old Philoctetes, the brave and vengeful Philoctetes of the island, must die, and with him the meaning of those years of bravery and suffering. The farewell to the island has a wealth of meaning,

> Farewell, Lemnos, sea-encircled,
> Blame me not but send me on my way
> With a fair voyage, to where a great destiny
> Carries me, and the judgment of friends and the all-conquering
> Spirit who has brought this to pass.

> [ll. 1463–68]

Oedipus at Colonus

The last, strangest, and perhaps most moving of Sophocles' tragedies was written when the dramatist was almost ninety and was produced in 402, after his death. For the third time—*Antigone* in

442, *Oedipus the King* in 427, and now *Oedipus at Colonus*—
Sophocles treated an aspect of the Theban legend. There are minor discrepancies in the three plots, but the figure of Oedipus in
the two plays called after him is certainly the same.

This play is a series of tableaux which progressively exhibits the
implications of this human, and soon to be divine, figure in his
last hours on earth. In virtue of his extraordinary history he has
been separated from the ordinary concerns of his fellow creatures
for almost half a lifetime. As the play opens, at what appears to
be an ordinary evening's halting place—Colonus—he receives "the
watchword of his destiny" (l. 46). He has stopped by the grove of
the Furies. Apollo has said that when he comes to his life's end,
he would find, in a place sacred to the Furies, his rest and abode,
and that this resting place of his, when his mortal life is over,
would be a protection to those that welcomed him and the bane
of his enemies who cast him out. Oedipus is filled with certainty
that this is the end of his journey, and the place where the final
meaning of his story—if meaning it is to be called—is going to
be written. "Yet I know this much: no sickness and no other
thing will kill me. I would not have been saved from death if not
for some strange evil fate," is how he had spoken of it in the
Oedipus the King (ll. 1455–58). At the moment of the discovery
and the blinding so many years ago, the end would naturally present itself as "some strange evil fate." It is not now so clear
whether it is good or evil, but it is the end, and Oedipus the man
finds that in the bestowal of his wretched carcass ("something
not truly very good to look at" [l. 577]) he has a gift of great
value. The light plays fitfully on the humanity of the man he still
is, and will soon cease to be; on his desire to break the barriers between this human world of his and his existence as a daemon the
other side of the gulf of death, by ensuring that his powers *then*
will be at the service of those chosen by the man *now;* on the last
moment before the disappearance and transformation, when he
feels that already these powers begin to be his. A plot in the sense
of a development, of a hinging of one event on the next, there

hardly is. But the action has a special tension of its own. It is the story of an either-or chance, which may succeed or fail. He may fail to convince the people of Colonus or their king to give shelter to the accursed suppliant. Creon's attempt to kidnap him and his daughters may be successful. This last, indeed, is the breaking point, where the feebleness of the old man imperils for the moment what is for him personally the value of the huge potency of the spirit that is to be. His grave—or the place of his disappearance from earth—is the source of his magic power. Can he have a say in who will own it? Is it to be at the service of his enemies as much as his friends? Is there to be nothing of Oedipus the sufferer to survive his last great trial?

This is another version of the various "Suppliants" plays with which we are familiar from the first Aeschylus to the last of Euripides. But there are interesting differences between this and the others. The Suppliants are always looking for a rescue from their pursuers and an asylum. This one is looking for the chance to invest his great destiny with a personal meaning—the meaning dictated by his view of his whole past life, and particularly his wrongs.[17] Thus it also looks toward *Philoctetes,* the play that directly preceded it. There the man of mysterious fate is compelled to surrender *all his humanity*—that is, *all* his sense of personal wrong and injury—to serve the impersonal destiny to which the gods have appointed him. Here the play is made to turn—as far as the plot goes—on the salvaging of something, on the right of the wronged to his human concept of vengeance; to the rewarding of his friends and the punishment of his enemies. His death or removal from this world is a fixed factor. This will happen anyhow. What concerns us as spectators is: will he have a personal triumph in it? Thus, special weight rests on the interview with Polyneices and the vividness of the hatred that flares for the last time. The destruction of his enemies has commenced.

The construction of the play falls into four parts. In the first, Oedipus establishes himself in his last bastion of defense by persuading the Chorus and Theseus to admit him. This is followed by two challenges. Creon tries to force Oedipus to return to Thebes—or rather some place convenient to the Theban border— by kidnapping his daughters. Polyneices tries to get his support and presence to help re-establish himself as prince of Thebes. In both these conflicts Oedipus is victorious. His daughters are restored to him by Theseus, and so this blackmail, which had not made a decisive impression on Oedipus anyway, loses what power it had. In the case of Polyneices, Oedipus refuses to see in him anyone different from the ungrateful son guilty of helping to expel his father. The last act is the solemn scene of the death, or transfiguration.

There is throughout a constant comparison of the attitude of Oedipus toward those around him (and theirs toward him), with his relation to the people of Thebes in his past, and perhaps to the hundreds of communities where he has stayed briefly since. What he expects to get and what he gets are now to be changed by the new fact of his imminent value as an impersonal power. It is, however, in doubt whether he can convince this community and this prince of the actual existence of this value of his. The first part of the play is therefore characterized by his own pleading of his case humanly, on the presentation of his innocence rationally considered. He is here a man among men, with the same emphasis on his innocence, for the Chorus who may be his protector, as in the dialogue with his enemy Creon. This attitude gives place to the gradual realization of himself as the possessor of power. As he gets back his daughters, as he realizes Polyneices' plight and knows that this is the working of his own curse against his hated son, the helpless blind beggar of the beginning is transformed before us into the terrifying near-spirit summoned by the thunder of Zeus to his last meeting place with the divinity that had pursued his life so relentlessly, branding it and setting it apart from that of others. In this, as in the other two plays I have chosen to discuss, the dramatist's main concern has been with the feelings of the man undergoing the transformation. The objective meaning of the transformation, and of the transformation of this particular man into a daemon, is there more by implication than anything else.

The first lines express the tired sense of the long, meaningless wandering that his life has been since he left Thebes:

> Child of the old blind man, Antigone,
> What country have we come to, what city of men?
> Who will receive me today
> With scantest gifts? Little indeed I ask
> Yet than that little I get less, but still
> What will content me. My sufferings
> And my long life have taught me to endure
> Yes, and nobility to make a third.

But when a passerby tells him that he has come to the grove of the Furies he knows that this is different from all other way-stations. This is the "watchword of his destiny." Here in some manner he does not yet know is the moment when "his life's scale shall turn in the balance" (l. 1508). Oedipus is looking for the course of that destiny, still to be charted. He only knows its watchword—the association with the Furies—and that he has a bargaining counter for his hosts. He can give them something for asylum.

This part of the play is mostly concerned with the political and social aspects of Oedipus' position. In fact, it is possible to describe the course of the plot as continuously narrowing and deepening as far as it illustrates Oedipus' relations to other men. First there is a whole community to placate, then the two enemies of the past to encounter in such a way that the advantages of the new ally are not thrown away; finally all that is left of human contact is his two daughters and the new stranger-protector whom he is making the heir of his last will and testament.

The community Oedipus confronts as a suppliant demanding

asylum is divided between the Chorus, expressing the mass of ordinary people, and Prince Theseus. On them Oedipus uses the arguments which he passionately feels should be convincing to a fellow human being. It is something like this: "I am not *consciously* a criminal. What I did was done in ignorance and was inflicted on me, especially by the powers outside of man, whose purposes and logic are not ours. This might happen to yourselves or anyone. Therefore, as men yourselves, you cannot in decency expel me." Also strengthened by the more exact knowledge of the oracles concerning the power of his grave, he offers his "wretched body" as a talisman against Theban victory in years to come. Theseus accepts. He does not at first imagine that the asylum granted the old man will cost him any political risk, but when those risks come he acts fairly and stands by his promise.

It is easy, at the beginning of the play, not to be aware of how fluid Oedipus' feelings still are. He becomes fixed in our minds as the figure of terror launching curses at his son with his latest breath. But, as the dramatist shows him at the start, he has been worn down to a great degree of patience by his years of wandering. Ismene tells him of the oracle which sets such high value on his grave. She tells him that Creon is coming to bring him from Athens (ll. 383–97). Why? "To put you near the land of Cadmus, so as to be master of you, without your setting foot on Theban soil."

"What advantage will I be to them if I lie *outside* the land?"

"Your burial place, if it *meet with ill luck,* will be dangerous to them."

"Anyone might know that without God's help."

"And so they wish to bring you near the country, and that you may not be your own master." Then follow the decisive two lines. Oedipus, in spite of his anger, has not yet quite determined what his enemies' course implies.

"And will they, then, shadow me in Theban dust?"

"No, the kinsman's blood you shed will not let them, father." Then he is certain.

"They will never own me, then" (ll. 406–8).

This interchange is vital for an understanding of the play's meaning. For Oedipus it is all important that the old sanctions, the blood-guilt and the incest, are still operative, at least in the minds of Creon and the Thebans. This carries him back in memory to the moment of his expulsion, and he decides once and for all never to make his peace with the rulers of Thebes that had enforced the gods' edicts against him. As Ismene's story continues he realizes his position of advantage as a source of power when dead, and he also believes that the quarrel of his sons, already started, is the first fruits of his curses on them, here and now. He accepts with bitterness and hope the realization which comes in the lines of Ismene, "In you, men say, lies victory for them." And Oedipus asks, "When I am nothing any more, am I a man?"

"Yes, for now the gods raise you up; before they ruined you."

"It is a poor thing to raise the old man that fell when young" (ll. 392–95).

The delicate shading of one mood into the other which finally spans the immense range from the humble old beggar to the savage arrogance of the nearly achieved divinity should not obscure certain implications of Oedipus' attitude to the men that drove him out and those who welcomed him.

As far as we can tell, the sanction that had banished Oedipus from Thebes is still in effect. Ismene believes so. Therefore Creon cannot in fact do anything but what he offers to do. It is true, of course, that his wish to have Oedipus near the boundary, and yet not over it, is typical of the instrumental use of another human being which Sophocles has already exhibited for our dislike in the treatment of Philoctetes by Odysseus in *Philoctetes*. But the rage of Oedipus is directed against Creon mainly because he cannot come back to Thebes. Yet in truth it hardly seems as though it lay in Creon's power to give him this permission; and in this nuance of the plot lie some strange meanings for the play.

The matter is blurred by Oedipus' remarkably clever pleading of his own case against his sons (ll. 427–49), who are alleged to have been guilty of his banishment. He says of the boys (and adds Creon along with them) that "had they expelled him at once after his blinding he would have welcomed it" (ll. 434–35). But they waited until the first wild rage and misery was over, when the victim was beginning to grow used to his world of darkness, and then they drove him from the only human home he had. At the end of *Oedipus the King* (which I do not think that Sophocles had forgotten) this period of delay is attributed to Creon's desire to consult Apollo again, now that the identity of Laius' murderer has been established. This would give a different color to the action with which Oedipus charges his persecutors. But this link with the earlier play need not be insisted on. It is easy to grant that Creon, and perhaps the boys, are shown as selfish and cruel. But it remains undeniable that Oedipus' banishment from Thebes begins and continues as a matter of divine enactment—expressed in the original oracle of Apollo. And to this extent Oedipus' fury against Creon is unjust. Furthermore, and bearing in the same direction, Oedipus' gratitude to Theseus is earned relatively easily. For now accepting him as a refugee does not involve risking the curse of the gods. On the contrary Oedipus comes, as he says himself, *hieros* ("holy"—under the protection of the gods when he sought shelter), *eusebes* ("pious"—perhaps more disputable), and bringing great benefits to the land where he resides. It is, of course, true that the Chorus and Theseus, had they accepted the more conventional conception of guilt and risk, might easily have thought it safer to turn him away. But, in fact, now the gods are on his side and the side of those who take him in. All Theseus has to do is to realize that this is so. No amount of realization on Creon's part, either earlier or presumably now, since Apollo's oracle still banished his body from Thebes, will make the curse inoperative. So allowing for all the human difference in attitude on the part of Theseus and Creon, allowing that Creon is selfish, politically minded, and unsympathetic in his treatment of Oedipus, and Theseus everything that is humane and enlightened, there is a notable want of concern with justice in Oedipus' attitude to the two.

In this it might be possible to see Oedipus, in Sophocles' presentation, rejecting the notion of ritual guilt, rejecting, that is, all guilt not consciously incurred by the criminal. Thus Oedipus would regard the decision of Creon and his sons to drive him out as cowardly and hypocritical. Theseus' acceptance of him as a suppliant is a proof of Theseus' enlightenment. (Theseus' position would then be much the same as he exhibits in Euripides' *Heracles Furens* at the end when he reassures Heracles about the contaminating power of his guilt [ll. 1311–39].) Such an interpretation would certainly give a clear and important meaning to Oedipus' pleading for his *essential* innocence to the Chorus, and to his rebuttals of Creon in the same spirit. It would make the theoretical positions underlying both *Oedipus the King* and *Oedipus at Colonus* really sharp in outline. Is it the correct view?

It seems to me that the weight of both plays is really against it. In both the earlier and the later play the horror of his unconscious acts has burned itself into Oedipus' soul. Of that nearly every speech bears witness. In *Oedipus at Colonus* his faith in the final alteration in his lot is not in the vindication of his innocence in the last stages of his life, but in the choice of the gods of himself as a portent in his last moments, as he had been through his miserable and suffering life. The fury with which he maintains his innocence before Creon is directed against the smugness of his fellow humans who ignore the arbitrariness of the divine control of man, and confuse acts, in which the "criminal" is entangled by the gods, with those for which, in any ordinary human context, he could be held responsible. Such folk ignore the warning given by Odysseus in *Ajax:* "Everything may happen when a god contrives." Surely if the conclusion of *Oedipus at Colonus* can be clearly interpreted at all, the interpretation runs in the direction of the mysterious and humanly inexplicable end of this man. The dramatist has done everything to emphasize the strangeness of this end. Both the crime and the final elevation to power are inexplicable. But Oedipus remains, of course, till his last moments, a human being with deep feelings and naturally these feelings are provoked by good and bad treatment. Yet the good and the bad treatment are controlled by the necessities imposed on man by divine direction. The relevance of human kindness and sympathy, above all the realization of our common human helplessness is all important, but its scope is contracted within narrow possibilities of action. Thus Oedipus' judgment that Creon is a hypocrite and calculating villain, and that Theseus is a generous and compassionate ruler is perfectly right, viewing them both as political authorities. But there lies behind this valid distinction the uncomfortable fact that Creon had to do what he did when Oedipus was expelled, and that Theseus did what he easily could when he accepted the old man into sanctuary. The difference, so important for Sophocles, lies in the tilting of the small balance. Creon would try to take the extreme advantage of someone whom circumstances put into a disadvantageous position; Theseus would stretch compassion a point or two beyond what is safe in a conventional course. This distinction is no less weighty because of the clear recognition of the role of necessity.

But the confusion in Oedipus' view of his enemies is also an important element in the presentation of the character. For Oedipus is on the road which will carry him from being a man to being one of those dimly understood but highly effective powers between god and man—the hero. He is trying to give his human wrongs in this world, his personal sufferings, a continued meaning—and therefore revenge—in the next. He contemplates with satisfaction the moment when "my long-buried cold corpse will drink the blood of my enemies" (ll. 621–22). He is, most emphatically not concerned with human justice and its relation to voluntariness and involuntariness—the very aspect he has urged on his own behalf earlier. He does not care whether Creon could have refrained from banishing him originally or could bring him back now. He is not moved by Theseus' barely veiled hint that he should treat his son Polyneices with some of the compassion bestowed on himself, as a suppliant and a stranger. He seizes on his new heroic powers to implement arbitrarily his heroic passions of hate and love. His enemies must be punished, his friends rewarded. To attain this, the satisfaction of a desire reaching from one world to the next, he must manipulate the brief span of days that lie in between.

Thus Oedipus' second act of confrontation with his past, his interview with Polyneices, is of still greater importance in developing the play's theme. It matches, in *Philoctetes,* the advance from the hero's victory over the brute force and deception of Odysseus to his no less absolute rejection of the friendly offer of Neoptolemos when the latter is urging the same course of action as the bully. This is the reason for the delicate shading, the ambiguity, in the representation of Polyneices. The dispassionate observer, Theseus, and the girls with their family loyalty, clearly think much better of him than of Creon. They clearly think that Oedipus should treat him better than he has Creon. The conversation between Polyneices and Antigone, when they are alone together and their father's terrible presence no longer holds them in constraint, betrays affection and concern on both sides. But none of this makes any difference to Oedipus. He discovers with savage joy that the power which is to be fully his after death has begun to operate. It is a slight foretaste but it comes when he is still human, when he can enjoy it. By this revenge he will forever establish the reality of the sequence of events which will lead his sons to their mutually inflicted deaths. With remarkable irony he sweeps away all the special pleading of Polyneices—the talk of repentance, retribution, any mitigating factor, all those human considerations which he had urged on his own behalf when dealing with the Chorus and Theseus. For now Oedipus can launch on others a curse the like of which has afflicted his own life. Now he is reaching toward the status of those divinities which control the career of humans with no concern other than the gratification of their own hates or loves. Here, at some level of mystical ambiguity, Sophocles presents the union of a totally human being suffused with the color of a god, a Greek god, whose incomprehensibility is momentarily comprehensible. For such a one the passion of anger, the resentment of wrong, is backed by power that fortunately does not belong to human beings. Justice has little to do with such a creature, for justice is peculiarly concerned with man's intentions, with this willingness or unwillingness, with what may be reasonably expected and what may not. The anger of the daemon is the source of potency; stir it and it falls alike on the just and on the unjust. Oedipus has been wronged by Creon and his sons. Given the opportunity he will destroy them, with no differentiation in their degree of guilt or any subjective consideration.

The last movement, as Oedipus goes to his meeting place with destiny, is the climax of the play. No other dramatist has tried anything exactly like this: to give dramatic shape to a moment for which there is no model in the acts of the human world. The placing of this scene, marked by an inhuman calm, right after the storm of the old man's anger against his son, the thunder and lightning, the parting from his daughters, his departure from the scene, and the account of the last parting of all, from Theseus, who, too, can accompany him no further, all express with extraordinary force the disembarrassment of everything human, the majesty of negation. Theseus' valediction runs:

> Those for whom night and darkness-under-earth
> Is but a stored-up grace, we should not mourn.
> To do so, brings God's anger on ourselves.

[ll. 1751–53]

Tragedy, or tragedy in its "best" version, as Aristotle understood it, this is not. It does not affect us with pity or fear for the hero—because he goes, not to a fitting disaster, but to a dubiously fitting triumph. But pity and fear in a more general sense, for the human condition, is perhaps evoked by the somber majesty of the last scenes. Oedipus sheds his human trappings, as he has laid aside his beggar's rags, as he waits for the lustral water fetched him by his daughter. He parts from the girls, to whom he has been bound so long with bonds of love and shame. The thunder and lightning warn of the apocalypse, and Oedipus' last anxiety is that Theseus, to whom he is to confide his secret, will find him dead or raving. For the weight of his secret is his last link with life, his last act of repayment in that god-controlled existence. As he has left his living curse to destroy his sons, he seeks opportunity for his last blessing to his new friends. These are the memorials of the reality of his life and its wrongs, the perpetuation for the generations to come of the sufferings and the final triumph of the god-doomed and god-exalted.

Notes

1. Herodotus viii. 121. The Greeks had sent to Salamis for the Aeacids and they arrived just at the outset of the battle (Her. viii. 64, 84). In *The Persians,* Aeschylus (who witnessed the battle) has Xerxes refer to Salamis as Ajax' isle (l. 369). On the cult of Ajax and the question of the right of burial see R. C. Jebb, *Sophocles, the Plays and Fragments,* 7: xxx–xxxii.

2. Cedric H. Whitman, *Sophocles: A Study of Heroic Humanism,* p. 79 and *passim.* Also see the following: C. M. Bowra (*Sophoclean Tragedy,* pp. 19–26) says, "[Sophocles'] Ajax is undeniably a real person . . . a character who was both a heroic being from a legendary past and a man whom the fifth century would understand from its own experience and by its own standards. Instead of copying the epic model he has recreated a heroic type and given it a new significance." T. B. L. Webster (*Introduction to Sophocles*) argues for free will (pp. 35–36) and says that the most important thing in the plays was the presentation of "a great figure" (p. 55).

3. Whitman, thinking of the Ajax trilogy of Aeschylus (*Judgment of*

Arms, The Trachian Women, and *The Women of Salamis*), remarks that Sophocles had been successful only in reducing the parts of the action from three to two (*Sophocles,* p. 63).

Webster describes the play as a "diptych," and, like Whitman, explains the plot by making reference to Aeschylus: "In the two earliest plays, Sophocles is still working in the Aeschylean tradition. Aeschylus wrote the Cassandra scene of the *Agamemnon* to prepare his audience for the end of the play and for the next play; Cassandra for the first time tells the story of Atreus, Thyestes, and Aegisthus, and prophesies the vengeance of Orestes. When Cassandra has entered the house, the first part of the *Agamemnon* ends with the death of the king." The overlapping scene, in this play, Webster thinks, is that which begins with the entry of Teucer's messenger and ends with the suicide of Ajax (*Introduction to Sophocles,* pp. 102–3).

Kitto says that the "unifying theme" of the play is not Ajax' sufferings but the antagonism between Ajax and Odysseus: "The end is rather the triumph of Odysseus than the rehabilitation of Ajax." He thinks that the conflict is between two "ethical conceptions": Ajax is wrong, Odysseus right (H. D. F. Kitto, *Greek Tragedy,* pp. 124–29 and 131–32).

Bowra says that the two halves develop two themes: "heavy wrong-doing" and "ultimate nobility." "The two are weighed against each other and in the end the nobility is seen to outweigh the faults" (*Sophoclean Tragedy,* pp. 18–19).

Waldock argues that the diptych shows the need for Greek drama to infuse a new "charge"—new energy—into the play. He takes issue with both Kitto and Bowra, saying that the latter's thematic explanation is inadequate—the first half of the play convinces us sufficiently of Ajax' nobility. He thinks that one's attentions in the second half are supposed to turn to the characters introduced there: Teucer and the Atreidae (A. J. A. Waldock, *Sophocles the Dramatist,* pp. 58–59, 61–67).

Jebb insists, on the other hand, that the play does have unity because the denial of burial rites stems from the main action and the question whether Ajax was to be given the status of a hero would have been of great importance to the audience (*Sophocles,* 7: xxviii–xxxii).

4. Bowra, *Sophoclean Tragedy,* pp. 43–44.

5. Ajax' bitterness is so great that when he meets Odysseus in the underworld, he stalks off without uttering a word, despite the latter's entreaties (*Odyssey* xi).

6. Bowra, *Sophoclean Tragedy,* pp. 17, 41, 49–60 *passim.*

7. "It seems impossible that Sophocles' innermost allegiance could have been to the official gods of Olympus, or that the heroic figures of his tragedies were created out of the straw of hybris in order to be knocked down as an object lesson in sophrosyne" (Whitman, *Sophocles,* p. 16; see also pp. 22–41 *passim* and pp. 67–69).

8. Lionel Abel, *Metatheatre: A New View of Dramatic Form*, pp. 2–5.

9. Bowra, *Sophoclean Tragedy*, pp. 43–44.

10. *Ibid*.

11. *Ajax*, ll. 834–39; *Prometheus Bound*, l. 515.

12. Bowra argues that *Electra, Oedipus at Colonus*, and *Ajax* also must be seen as "happy ending" plays (*Sophoclean Tragedy*, pp. 359–60).

13. The Sather Lectures of Professor Bernard Knox (*The Heroic Temper*) appeared when I had completed the Sophocles essays and indeed nearly this entire volume. I am aware of the great similarity in our interpretation especially in regard to *Philoctetes*, but despair of including enough footnotes to cover the similarities and differences. I trust he will regard this as an acknowledgment of my pleasure at so many of the points of agreement between us.

14. Edmund Wilson believes Neoptolemos is in fact at the center of the play: "How then is the gulf to be got over between the ineffective plight of the bowman and his proper use of the bow, between his ignominy and his destined glory? Only by the intervention of one who is guileless enough and human enough to treat him not as a monster, nor yet as a mere magical property which is wanted for some end, but simply as another man, whose sufferings elicit his sympathy and whose courage and pride he admires. . . . In taking the risk to his cause which is involved in the recognition of his common humanity with the sick man . . . he dissolves Philoctetes' stubbornness and thus cures him and sets him free, and saves the campaign as well" (Edmund Wilson, *The Wound and the Bow*, p. 295).

15. What we are seeking here is what Lucian meant in his definition of the hero:

"Menippus: What is a hero?

"Trophonius: A mixture of man and god.

"Menippus: So what's neither man nor god, so you say, is both together" (Lucian, *Dialogues of the Dead* 3.2).

16. For a different interpretation of the figure of Odysseus see Bowra (*Sophoclean Tragedy*, pp. 284–89). Bowra thinks the two representations very dissimilar. In *Philoctetes*, Odysseus is dishonest, hypocritical, and ambitious—an exemplar of the sort of mentality Thucydides describes in the chapter on stasis (iii. 82). When he quits the stage in *Philoctetes*, Bowra says, "his failure is complete. It is clear the gods will not work through agents like him." In *Ajax*, he thinks, Odysseus is "a model of courtesy and courage" (p. 331).

Compare also with Whitman (*Sophocles*, p. 71) who remarks that in *Ajax*, Odysseus "behaves with perfect civilization and decency."

17. See Bowra, *Sophoclean Tragedy*, pp. 330–39.

SELECTED BIBLIOGRAPHY

NOTE: The translations from the Greek plays are my own. In quoting from those tragedies that I personally translated for the *Complete Greek Tragedies,* published by the University of Chicago Press, I have used the printed versions. In quotations from the rest I have translated the passages as I have needed them for this book.

Abel, Lionel. *Metatheatre: A New View of Dramatic Form.* New York: Hill & Wang, 1963.

Bowra, C. M. *Sophoclean Tragedy.* Oxford: Clarendon Press, 1944.

Jebb, R. C. *Sophocles, the Plays and Fragments.* 8 vols. Amsterdam: Servio, 1962.

Kitto, H. D. F. *Greek Tragedy.* Garden City, N.Y.: Doubleday Anchor Books, 1954.

Knox, Bernard. *The Heroic Temper.* Berkeley and Los Angeles: University of California Press, 1964.

Letters, Francis Joseph Henry. *The Life and Work of Sophocles.* New York: Sheed & Ward, 1953.

Reinhardt, Karl. *Sophokles.* Frankfurt am Main: V. Klostermann, 1933.

Waldock, A. J. A. *Sophocles the Dramatist.* Cambridge: University Press, 1951.

Webster, T. B. L. *Introduction to Sophocles.* Oxford: Clarendon Press, 1944.

Weinstock, Heinrich. *Sophokles.* 3d revised edition. Wuppertal: Marées-Verlag, 1948.

Whitman, Cedric H. *Sophocles: A Study of Heroic Humanism.* Cambridge: Harvard University Press, 1951.

Wilamowitz-Moellendorff, Tycho von. *Die dramatische technik de Sophokles.* Philologische Untersuchungen, Heft 22, 1917.

Wilson, Edmund. *The Wound and the Bow.* Cambridge: Riverside Press, 1941.